STUDIES IN ENGLISH LITERATURE No. 73

General Editor

David Daiches

Already published in the series:

1. **Milton:** Comus *and* Samson Agonistes
by *J. B. Broadbent*
2. **Pope:** The Rape of the Lock
by *J. S. Cunningham*
3. **Jane Austen:** Emma
by *Frank Bradbrook*
4. **W. B. Yeats:** The Poems
by *A. Norman Jeffares*
5. **Chaucer:** The Knight's Tale *and*
The Clerk's Tale
by *Elizabeth Salter*
6. **Marlowe:** Dr Faustus
by *J. P. Brockbank*
7. **Hardy:** The Mayor of Casterbridge
by *Douglas Brown*
8. **Webster:** The Duchess of Malfi
by *Clifford Leech*
10. **Wordsworth:** The Prelude and
other poems by *John F. Danby*
11. **George Eliot:** Middlemarch
by *David Daiches*
12. **Conrad:** Lord Jim
by *Tony Tanner*
13. **Shakespeare:** Hamlet
by *Kenneth Muir*
14. **Shakespeare:** Macbeth
by *John Russell Brown*
15. **Shakespeare:** King Lear
by *Nicholas Brooke*
16. **Shakespeare:** Much Ado About Nothing
by *J. R. Mulryne*
17. **Donne:** Songs and Sonets
by *A. J. Smith*
18. **Marvell:** Poems
by *Dennis Davison*
19. **Dickens:** Great Expectations
by *R. George Thomas*
20. **Emily Brontë:** Wuthering Heights
by *Frank Goodridge*
21. **Shakespeare:** The Merchant of Venice
by *A. D. Moody*

24. **Shakespeare:** Henry IV
by *R. J. Beck*
25. **Shakespeare:** As You Like It
by *Michael Jamieson*
26. **Shakespeare:** The Winter's Tale
by *A. D. Nuttall*
28. **D. H. Lawrence:** Sons and Lovers
by *Gamini Salgado*
29. **Dickens:** Little Dorrit
by *J. C. Reid*
30. **E. M. Forster:** A Passage to India
by *John Colmer*
31. **Shakespeare:** Richard II
by *A. R. Humphreys*
32. **Henry James:** The Portrait of a Lady
by *David Galloway*
34. **Blake:** The Lyric Poetry
by *John Holloway*
35. **Shakespeare:** A Midsummer Night's
Dream
by *Stephen Fender*
36. **Mark Twain:** Huckleberry Finn
by *Jonathan Raban*
37. **T. S. Eliot:** The Waste Land
by *Helen Williams (2nd edition)*
38. **Swift:** Gulliver's Travels
by *Angus Ross*
39. **Shakespeare:** The Tempest
by *John Russell Brown*
40. **Conrad:** Nostromo
by *Juliet McLauchlan*
42. **Golding:** Lord of the Files
by *John S. Whitley*
43. **Hardy:** Tess of the D'Urbervilles
by *Bruce Hugman*
44. **Shakespeare:** Antony and Cleopatra
by *Robin Lee*
45. **Webster:** The White Devil
by *D. C. Gunby*
46. **D. H. Lawrence:** The Rainbow
by *Frank Glover-Smith*

Already published in the series (*continued*):

47. **Shakespeare:** Othello
    by *Juliet Mclauchlan*

48. **Virginia Woolf:** To be Lighthouse
    by *Stella McNichol*

49. **Pope:** The Dunciad
    by *Howard Erskine-Hill*

50. **James Joyce:** Ulysses
    by *Michael Mason*

51. **Tobias Smollett:**
    The Expedition of Humphry Clinker
    by *John Valdimir Price*

52. **James Joyce:**
    A Portrait of the Artist as a Young Man
    by *Harvey Peter Sucksmith*

53. **Gerard Manley Hopkins:** The Poems
    by *R. K. R. Thornton*

54. **Dickens:** Bleak House
    by *Grahame Smith*

55. **Samuel Richardson:** Clarissa
    by *Anthony Kearney*

56. **Wordsworth and Coleridge:**
    The Lyrical Ballads
    by *Stephen Prickett*

57. **Shakespeare:** Measure for Measure
    by *Nigel Alexander*

58. **Shakespeare:** Coriolanus
    by *Brian Vickers*

59. **Chaucer:** Troilus and Criseyde
    by *A. C. Spearing*

60. **F. Scott Fitzgerald:** The Great Gatsby
    by *John S. Whitley*

61. **John Gay:** The Beggar's Opera
    by *Peter Lewis*

62. **Patrick White:** Voss
    by *William Walsh*

63. **Huxley and Orwell:** Brave New
    World *and* Nineteen Eighty-Four
    by *Jenni Calder*

64. Poetry of the First World War
    by *J. M. Gregson*

65. **Shakespeare:** Julius Caesar
    by *David Daiches*

67. **Dickens:** David Copperfield
    by *Phillip Collins*

68. **Tourneur:** The Revenger's Tragedy
    by *Philip J. Ayres*

69. **Melville:** Moby Dick
    by *Brian Way*

70. Beowulf
    by *T. A. Shippey*

71. **Shakespeare:** Richard III
    by *D.C. Gunby*

72. **Shakespeare:** Twelfth Night
    by *J.M. Gregson*

73. **Congreve:** The Way of the World
    by *Malcolm Kelsall*

CONGREVE: THE WAY OF THE WORLD

by

Malcolm Kelsall

Professor of English
University College, Cardiff

EDWARD ARNOLD

© Malcolm Kelsall 1981

First published 1981 by
Edward Arnold (Publishers) Ltd
41 Bedford Square
London WC1B 3DQ

British Library Cataloguing in Publication Data

Kelsall, Malcolm Miles
  Congreve 'The way of the world'.—(Studies in
  English literature; no. 73).
  1. Congreve, William, 1670 – 1729. The way of the world
  I. Title   II. Series
  822.5   PR3364.W33

  ISBN 0 7131 6342 9

Printed and bound in Great Britain at
The Camelot Press Ltd,
Southampton

General Preface

The object of this series is to provide studies of individual novels, plays and groups of poems and essays which are known to be widely read by students. The emphasis is on clarification and evaluation; biographical and historical facts, while they may be discussed when they throw light on particular elements in a writer's work, are generally subordinated to critical discussion. What kind of work is this? What exactly goes on here? How good is this work, and why? These are the questions that each writer will try to answer.

It should be emphasized that these studies are written on the assumption that the reader has already read carefully the work discussed. The objective is not to enable students to deliver opinions about works they have not read, nor is it to provide ready-made ideas to be applied to works that have been read. In one sense all critical interpretation can be regarded as foisting opinions on readers, but to accept this is to deny the advantages of any sort of critical discussion directed at students or indeed at anybody else. The aim of these studies is to provide what Coleridge called in another context 'aids to reflection' about the works discussed. The interpretations are offered as suggestive rather than as definitive, in the hope of stimulating the reader into developing further his own insights. This is after all the function of all critical discourse among sensible people.

Because of the interest which this kind of study has aroused, it has been decided to extend it first from merely English literature to include also some selected works of American literature and now further to include selected works in English by Commonwealth writers. The criterion will remain that the book studied is important in itself and is widely read by students.

DAVID DAICHES

Contents

Foreword

1. Hero and villain: I. 1-95   9

2. Two mistresses: II. 1 – 290   17

3. The heroine: II. 291 – 451   30

4. The proposal of marriage: IV. 60 – 289   38

5. 'Female frailty': the role and function of Lady Wishfort   47

6. The denouement: Act V   53

Notes   60

Further reading   62

Index   63

Foreword

The complexity of speech and action is the main cause both of the richness and of the difficulty of *The Way of the World*. The first step towards understanding the play must be through analysis of the dialogue. The style of utterance is compact and rich, and theatrical interpretation of this work fundamentally rests on the density of meaning in what is said and (more subtly) what is not said. Close attention must therefore be given to questions of tone, the use of innuendo and ambiguity, the shadings and shifts of vocabulary, the level of seriousness with which speeches should be judged, the interplay between naturalness and convention. From the very beginning the ear must rapidly accommodate itself to nuances of expression and tone, to ambiguity and evasion in argument, and to a speed and perplexity of advance which is exhilarating but also continually intellectually demanding. No time is offered to gradually 'tune in', yet, until the ear has adjusted to the latent as well as obvious elements of the dialogue, the audience will be lost. Such confusion is part of the intrinsic method, however, of a work concerned with strategem, treachery and disguise. The notoriously difficult and artificial plot has to be followed through dialogue which is often indirect, and in the relationships of characters who are frequently not what they seem.

But is it proper to treat in the same way all the strategies of concealment? The double-dealing Machiavellianism of Mirabell against Fainall in its mechanisms suggests something closer to the manner of melodrama. The business of Lady Wishfort resembles the exaggerated humours of Jonsonian comedy. The counterpointing is nice since unity of structure compels blending of modes, and a common artificiality of social behaviour and verbal dexterity in speech conceals transitions. Yet to play the piece as a brilliant display of manners would devalue the strong (and near tragic) passions always liable to press against and through verbal decorum, while, on the other hand, to play it 'for real' would merely highlight the extreme staginess of the plot and the contrived situations.

Congreve expressed surprise that *The Way of the World* succeeded on the stage, and Sir Richard Steele claimed in his 'Commendatory Verses' that the play was directed only 'to the few refined'. This seems to acknowledge that the play is not easy. Yet once the subtlety of the method is apprehended, even the best work of Congreve's contemporaries appears simplistic in comparison.

1. Hero and villain: I. 1 – 95[1]

In the opening scene it is unlikely that the audience will immediately discriminate between Mirabell and Mr Fainall as the 'hero' and 'villain' of the piece. Nothing they say would necessarily lead to that conclusion. Their language is equally matched in elegance and intelligence. In the first production the ambiguity would have been enhanced, for Mr Fainall was played by Betterton, the leading actor of the company, and the romantic lover of Congreve's previous comedy: *Love for Love* (1695). Perhaps there is a darkish hint in the very first line: 'You are a fortunate man, Mr Fainall' – for his name is an obvious label. But it may suggest no more than that he is a delightful libertine who misleads the ladies, and the ethical standards of Restoration comedy would not condemn a rake who might seduce without detection. The hero of Wycherley's *The Country Wife* is called Horner, which is cruder in suggestion without necessarily implying condemnation. Meantime the name of Mr Fainall's antagonist at cards is deliberately witheld for some minutes. Only on the entry of Witwoud are we given the positive signal that this other gentleman is called 'Mirabell', but that need only imply that he is handsome.

We might suppose, therefore, that we are in the presence of conventional heroes of comedy of the time: libertine men of the town whose pleasure is love and money, and whose conversation turns on marriage (with a fortune) or seduction (without scandal).[2] Mr Fainall describes his unnamed companion (Mirabell) as his 'friend'. The only possible reason for doubting that might lie in the uneasy tone of the conversation, and the fact that Mirabell does not use the term 'friend' himself. We shall learn later how devalued that word has become.

The Restoration comic norm to which the scene approximates may be illustrated by the exchanges between Bellmour and Vainlove in Congreve's first comedy *The Old Bachelor* (1693):

Bellmour   Vainlove, and abroad so early! Good morrow. I thought a contemplative lover could no more have parted with his bed in a morning, than he could have slept in't.

> *Vainlove*   Bellmour, good morrow. Why, truth on't is, these early
> sallies are not usual to me, but business, as you see, sir − (*Showing
> letters*). And business must be followed, or be lost.
> *Bellmour*   Business! And so must time, my friend, be close pursued,
> or lost. Business is the rub of life, perverts our aim, casts off the bias,
> and leaves us wide and short of the intended mark.
> *Vainlove*   Pleasure, I guess you mean.
> *Bellmour*   Ay, what else has meaning?

Thematically this exchange touches one of the major themes of the
comedy of the age: that popular epicureanism which had turned a refined
philosophical system into simple hedonism, especially the pursuit of
sexual pleasure, with its motto *carpe diem* − live for the pleasures of today
and take no thought of tomorrow. This theme has echoes in the dialogue
of Mr Fainall and Mirabell. But dramatically the disagreement between
Bellmour and Vainlove is of no major signification in the development of
The Old Bachelor and the dialogue does little to advance the action. On the
other hand, in *The Way of the World*, there is a latent element of tension
in the polite exchanges of Mr Fainall and Mirabell which is the seed from
which the major conflict of these two protagonists will develop. We
have no means of knowing that *Mrs* Fainall is Mirabell's discarded
mistress married off to Mr Fainall when she and Mirabell feared she was
pregnant. Nor can we foresee the role of Mr Fainall's own mistress,
Marwood, whose jealous and unrequited desire for Mirabell precipitates
disaster. Yet the existence of these relationships − which we will learn
later − must colour the dialogue of the two men who are very far from
'friends'. Although it is scarcely detectable, there is, from the beginning,
hostility between them.

The game of cards between hero and villain − on which the curtain
rises − serves as an icon of this hostility. It is a mimic warfare codified to
rules, in this reflecting the formality and artificiality of the social conflicts
in which the two men will be engaged. Yet, although it is an appropriate
image, it would be difficult to sharpen the card playing with a more
sinister edge in practical production in the theatre, because Mirabell
obviously does not have his mind on *that* game. What we detect is an
element of unease in him, manifesting itself in potential ill-temper.
'Prithee, why so reserved?' Fainall asks. 'Something has put you out of
humour'. Perhaps this arises from nothing more than Mirabell's quarrel

with Millamant, and the flicker of antagonism between the two men is exquisitely masked in the elegant decorums of verbal politeness. Yet, is there not a possible barb even in the first line, the tone of which is problematical? 'You are a fortunate man, Mr Fainall' seems to allude to the old saying: lucky at cards, unlucky in love, and so many suggestions lurk just beneath the surface of Mirabell's discourse, he may here be alluding to Mr Fainall's disastrous marriage. Likewise there may be an element of *Schadenfreude* (delight in mischief) in Mr Fainall's inopportune probing, 'Confess, Millamant and you quarrelled last night.' It is difficult to avoid the implication that one cause why Mr Fainall is 'gay' is that Mirabell is 'grave'. Only later will we learn, however, that Mr Fainall has another, more mercenary motive for his offensive curiosity disguised as banter. If Millamant marries without Lady Wishfort's (her aunt's) consent, Mr Fainall stands to gain half her fortune through his wife (Lady Wishfort's daughter).

There is little to choose between the two men at this juncture, however. Mirabell is just as interested in Millamant's money as his antagonist is. His 'sham addresses' to Lady Wishfort, behind which he has masked his advances to her daughter, are a clear instance of 'feigning'. He is not quite the same kind of rake as the other man, however. Mr Fainall announces his libertine code thus: 'I'd no more play with a man that slighted his ill fortune than I'd make love to a woman who undervalued the loss of her reputation', which seems to draw a polite moral rebuke from Mirabell upon its too exquisite epicureanism: 'You have a taste extremely delicate and are for refining on your pleasures.' Yet Mirabell's marrying off his supposedly pregnant mistress to the other man, if it does not refine upon his pleasure, shows a most peculiar regard for 'loss of . . . reputation'.

It would be a matter of the nicest moral casuistry, therefore, to distinguish hero and villain at the beginning, although, by the end, they will be far removed from one another. In Mirabell's favour we shall discover that his relation with Mrs Fainall has far more genuine concern in it than is implied in Mr Fainall's expression 'make love', which is a periphrasis merely for the sexual act, and that the lady herself was a young, amorous widow and thus knew what she was about! Nobody in 'the world' in this play blames Mirabell for this affair, least of all the lady in question. Concerning Lady Wishfort: although Mirabell merely passes off as a joke the word 'virtue' – which forbade him to seduce *her* – (what he implies is that she was too old and ugly to arouse him), nonetheless there is some moral principle here. He is, in any case, now honourably courting a woman he wishes to marry for love (and money). Mr Fainall's views on promiscuity, on the other hand, come from a man who is already married, and there is a distinction to be made between sex before marriage, and sex outside marriage. Admittedly such discrimination will not carry much weight with any critic of the ethos of Restoration comedy who sets a high value on chastity, but judged by the standards which obtain within that kind of comedy, Mirabell is very far from a rakish hero whose virility is measured by his sexual capacity. Even 'noble' and 'generous' Valentine in the more romantic *Love for Love* had a bastard son whom he wishes smothered by the whore his mother.

On the other hand, the very proximity of Mr Fainall and Mirabell should induce at least a certain scepticism before the claim sometimes advanced that Mirabell is Congreve's 'ideal' gentleman. Nothing in the play, including even Millamant's attitude to her lover and husband, indicates that intelligent, worldly people think in terms of such ideals. Moreover, Congreve's observations on his creation of comic characters contain no hints of such absolutes. On the contrary, he wrote that he thought in terms of 'mixed' personality in his protagonists, and what he claimed of Valentine in *Love for Love* fits Mirabell well enough:

> the Character is a mix'd Character; his Faults are fewer than his good Qualities; and, as the World goes, he may pass well enough for the best Character in a Comedy; where even the best must be shewn to have Faults, that the best Spectators may be warn'd not to think too well of themselves. [3]

This observation derives ultimately from Aristotle's definition of the genre, [4] and in assessing the sexuality of the protagonist one must bear in mind that sexual promiscuity has always been among the venial faults of the young in comedy. It is a point made by François Hédélin who seems to have been one of Congreve's mentors on the theory of the stage. [5]

Rather than considering the hero of the play as an 'ideal', there may well be a better case for seeing in him Congreve's attempt at a rare combination: Machiavellianism and virtue. Comedy has many protagonists of machinating skill, sharpness and wit – consider Barabas in *The Jew of Malta* or Volpone – but they often end by alienating our sympathy, and are punished. The best example of a wicked Machiavellian protagonist in

Congreve's own work is Maskwell in *The Double Dealer* (1693) who is more sinister than Mr Fainall. A problem in that work is that the darkness of Maskwell's duplicity introduces elements of tragedy and/or melodrama which do not easily fit the comedy, and the hero – Mellefont – runs the danger of appearing little more than a sentimental example of gullibility by comparison. Cynthia, the heroine, seems to be looking for both virtue and skillful manipulation of events in her lover when she says to Mellefont: 'since I consent to like a man without the vile consideration of money, he should give me a very evident demonstration of his wit' (IV.i), but Mellefont is so comprehensively fooled by his seeming friend, the knave, Maskwell, that proof of his wit is singularly lacking.

In *Love for Love* Valentine demonstrates his sincerity by proving that Angelica's person, not her fortune, was his aim, but here too his 'wit' is often a source of ridicule. His one 'mask' – his pretence to have gone out of his mind – is at once seen through by the sharp eyes of Angelica, and his pretention to literary wit is derided by his practical servant Jeremy. Valentine is an amiable young man, but compared with Mirabell he is not well fitted to survive in the shark-infested waters of this world.

Possibly Congreve is attempting in *The Way of the World* the difficult task of depicting the kind of manipulative wit that Cynthia demanded but did not find in Mellefont. Mirabell has sufficient skill in 'feigning' to win his mistress against every form of counterplot, yet sufficient integrity and charm to be desirable. Inevitably, therefore, the hero of *The Way of the World* will recall Maskwell, and the dramatic strategy is to pair him with another hypocrite – Mr Fainall – onto whom all the ill qualities of Machiavellianism in comic theatre can be projected. Thus the two men must occupy a certain amount of common ground, and in their early exchanges may not easily be distinguished. The antagonism of the 'friends' is not only dramatically exciting from the beginning, it is also structurally crucial. In following the thrusts and ripostes of the verbal fencing of the opening scene one must consider, therefore, both how Mirabell establishes a comparative moral superiority over Mr Fainall (however slight), and how he gets off the defensive and at last establishes sufficient advantage over his antagonist to make Mr Fainall cry off the match: 'Fie, fie, friend! If you grow censorious, I must leave you.' The subtlety and quickness with which this is done is at times so deft that (like foils) it is deceptive. Consider the exchange after Mirabell's admission that his 'evil genius' – Lady Wishfort – by coming in had spoiled his evening:

Fainall Oh, there it is then! She has a lasting passion for you, and
with reason. What, then my wife was there?
Mirabell Yes, and Mrs Marwood and three or four more, whom I
never saw before.

Mr Fainall's speech carries the possible innuendo that Mirabell has had a
sexual liaison with Lady Wishfort (the audience are not given the hero's
denial until later), just as, shortly, he will suggest that Mirabell has a
shrewd eye on Millamant's fortune. Presumably there must be a short
pause before he changes the subject to his wife, and since Mirabell has not
interjected an answer to Mr Fainall's innuendo there may be a hint that he
has 'scored' here. It would be psychologically apposite that the relaxation
which success engenders betrays him into a careless remark. His next
sentence reveals that he does not know where his wife was last evening,
and does not much care – which at once prompts Mirabell's loaded 'and
Mrs Marwood'. It is the one name he picks out from the cabal of ladies,
and it is not an accidental choice. Mirabell perhaps knows, certainly
suspects, that Marwood is Mr Fainall's mistress, just as he knows that she
has betrayed him to Lady Wishfort. He must accordingly suspect that
Marwood's lover may be in league against him.

It is impossible for an audience to deduce this from what can only be
the slightest loading of some innuendo on 'and Mrs Marwood'. Yet, in
the real world about us, it is precisely by catching hints and overtones
that we learn to 'read' people and situations, however tentatively, and
the audience will pick up, marginally, that there is something special
about this name. It occurs a second time in this episode, relating to the
discovery of Mirabell's real motives in courting Lady Wishfort: 'for the
discovery of that amour, I am indebted to your friend, or your wife's
friend, Mrs Marwood.' This time the innuendo is much clearer, and Mirabell pursues his advantage until Mr Fainall is forced to quit the room.

By 'your friend' Mirabell means 'mistress'. The *précieux* language of
idealism in this play is always suspect,[6] and Mirabell's ironically polite
back-tracking on his expression to 'or your wife's friend' should provide
sufficient emphasis on the word to make the audience suspicious, even if
it missed the first innuendo of 'and Mrs Marwood'. What we are to
make of a man's mistress being his wife's friend must remain problematical. Is Mrs Marwood sincere in her regard for Mrs Fainall? That seems
unlikely. If she is insincere, then 'friendship' is a screen for deceit. A

relationship with the wife will provide cover for access to the husband. Yet, since even an outsider like Mirabell has guessed at this, is Mrs Fainall so foolish as not to be aware herself what is going on, and if she is aware, what are her reasons for tolerating the 'friendship'? Far more questions are being raised at this moment than the mind has time consciously to formulate, let alone sift. They will not begin to be answered until the second act, but the irony, innuendo, and obliqueness of the dialogue has an unsettling effect. Suspicion is aroused. The value of words and professions becomes uncertain. Yet the audience is denied sufficient information to understand what is occurring. The technique resembles that of the novels of Henry James, but it is also like life itself in so far as it is by the same imperfect ways one seeks to understand any unfamiliar situation.

Mr Fainall advances a true explanation (though by way of rhetorical question) at this point of Marwood's hostility to Mirabell: Mirabell has rejected her advances. This we will learn is true. But it is in keeping with the dissimulation of the play that Mirabell entirely denies the matter, putting it down to 'good manners'. The *tone* in which he does so, however, seems to indicate to Mr Fainall that Mirabell in fact *admits* some sort of liaison, so that ambiguities multiply:

> *Fainall*   You are a gallant man, Mirabell; and though you may have cruelty enough not to satisfy a lady's longing, you have too much generosity not to be tender of her honour. Yet you speak with an indifference which seems to be affected, and confesses you are conscious of a negligence.

The language of courtly love here is potentially debased: 'gallant', 'cruelty', 'generosity', 'honour' – these words are a glittering wrapping to give to what is no more than a failed promiscuous pass. Mr Fainall presses the matter with importunate curiosity, and Mirabell's swift counter drives him out of the room and hence confirms the earlier innuendos concerning Marwood:

> *Mirabell*   You pursue the argument with a distrust that seems to be unaffected, and confesses you are conscious of a concern for which the lady is more indebted to you than your wife.

Mirabell 'wins' the verbal exchange, therefore, which matters more than the game of cards, and he wins it with a certain amount of honour.

Mr Fainall has revealed, at least to Mirabell's astute intelligence, that he and Marwood are indeed engaged in an affair. This is some sort of counter to the revelation of his own dissembling with Lady Wishfort, and is potentially a 'hold' on the dangerous Marwood, and on Mr Fainall. If either of them interferes in his designs again, the implication is that Mirabell has scandalous insight which he may deploy against them. As we shall see, the end of the play turns on this revelation.

Two major items of information are still witheld in a complex situation: we know nothing of Mirabell's liaison with Mrs Fainall, nor that Mr Fainall has excellent financial reasons for wishing Marwood *not* to come between Mirabell and Millamant. The villain and villainess, therefore, are working against one another, which is a serious weakness in their position, and one cause of their violent and deeply disturbing quarrel in the second act. Another important matter still remains unclear: how much does Millamant's money matter to Mirabell? Is he a fortune hunter, and how truly is he in love? Even Valentine in *Love for Love* was suspected by Angelica, and Mirabell is a much cleverer dissembler. We should not sentimentalize him. Millamant never does. It is made abundantly clear that she does not trust him, and is alarmed at finding herself in love.

If the action of the play were to continue at the same level of implication and innuendo as this opening exchange between Mirabell and Mr Fainall, it is unlikely that any audience could keep pace. Probably, for many, merely to grasp the outline of the plot is sufficiently taxing, a matter perversely confused, it seems, by the bewildering familial inter-relationships. Almost everyone in this play is related.

The introduction of Witwoud and Petulant, therefore, serves as a relaxation. From two arch dissemblers we move to a couple of easily read 'affected' characters (Congreve's own term), ultimately originating from Jonsonian comic tradition, though possibly more directly derived from Cutter and Worm in Cowley's *The Cutter of Coleman Street* (1661). They serve functionally like the clowns in any Elizabethan play, and the change of convention is reflected by a change to a far more broad and open style of writing. *The Way of the World* mixes dramatic modes, but the play's interleaving of different generic devices is a matter of such general importance as to merit separate consideration. The rivalry of Mirabell and Mr Fainall still requires further elucidation. Let us advance, therefore, to the beginning of the second act when the mistresses of the two men are introduced, first alone, then briefly in quartet, then each paired with her lover.

2. Two mistresses: II. 1 – 290

The entry of Mrs Fainall and Marwood parallels the introduction of Mr Fainall and Mirabell. It is not clear which of the women will emerge as the 'villainess' of the piece. Both of them, like the men, are dissembling, both probing for information from the other 'friend'. Congreve even repeats the device of revealing immediately the name of one of them: 'Aye, aye, dear Marwood' – while the name of the other is concealed until she sees her detested husband. (The tone of 'dear' is possibly exaggerated by affectation, for it is insincere, as is all their conversation.) Marwood, like Mr Fainall her lover, also makes a profession of 'libertine' sentiment: 'For my part, my youth may wear and waste, but it shall never rust in my possession'. The two rakes are thus united in their (villainous) progress.

Mrs Fainall's opening lines have an important and mordant application to the world of the play, and to Restoration comedy in general:

> Men are ever in extremes, either doting or averse. While they are lovers, if they have fire and sense, their jealousies are insupportable. And when they cease to love (we ought to think at least) they loathe; they look upon us with horror and distaste; they meet us like the ghosts of what we were, and as such, fly from us.

Although the initial discussion on mankind is soon said by the participants to be dissembled, and its abstraction proves to be beside the immediate dramatic issue, yet its pessimism colours much of the comedy. The relationship between Marwood and Mr Fainall so exactly fits the pattern that it is possible that Mrs Fainall alludes to the matter. Millamant's fear of Mirabell derives in part from a suspicion that he loves her because he has not had her, and when he has, he will come to loathe her. The state of matrimony by promoting familiarity breeds contempt and infidelity. The fate of a woman in this play world is all too frequently that of either hated wife or cast mistress. Hence the famous proviso scene in which Millamant and Mirabell bargain to avoid such a situation. One of the good qualities of Congreve's hero, in comparison with Mr Fainall, is that he is capable of care and respect even when he has ceased to love. His relationship with his cast mistress, Mrs Fainall, is tender, but it is the exception rather than the rule. These matters will require fuller examination later.

The problem as seen by the women is that Nature compels them to the dotage of love, and the longing for pleasure which tyrannizes them leads to situations which will end in pain. Marwood's description of this paradox, though elaborately distanced in artificial discourse, suggests a situation closer to tragedy than comedy. Her description of marriage as a relationship she desires, because it will enable her to torment her husband with jealousy, is sufficiently bizarre as to be comic, yet suggests also the pathological perversity of a mind corrupted by a frustrated passion she loathes as much as she enjoys. The elegant brilliance of her argument is a phosphorescence of spiritual decay. Maybe she is only playing with such ideas, but that she entertains them at all is an indication of her sickness. As Mirabell remarked of Mr Fainall, this is 'refining' on one's pleasures. There is much in *The Way of the World* which is bleak and darkly satirical, and the happy resolution for Congreve's true lovers has to be won from the jaws of adversity. One thinks of the tragi-comedies of Shakespeare.

Like Mirabell and Mr Fainall, the two women are fishing for useful information. Both wish to know how the other feels towards Mirabell. When Marwood 'professes' herself as 'libertine' she continues:

> You see my friendship by my freedom. Come, be as sincere, acknowledge that your sentiments agree with mine.

The word 'friendship' here — as so often in the play — is bogus, and the claim of sincerity is the mask of dissimulation (it was the favourite device of Maskwell in *The Double Dealer*). The bait is offered so that Mrs Fainall will exchange confidence for confidence, and reveal whether she has a lover. When she remains firm on her position that she hates mankind 'heartily, inveterately' — and her husband particularly — Marwood at once backs down from her own exposed 'sincere' position, for she might be asked to confide in turn. She retreats with a highly stagey observation: 'What I have said has been to try you.' This is rarely a convincing dramatic device, and the women's dialogue at this point seems a little stilted. Perhaps this is a stylistic means of indicating a discrepancy between what they are and what they 'profess'. There is not the natural ease of the original conversation between Mirabell and Mr Fainall, and it may be that Congreve is suggesting that the women are not so skilled in dissimulation as the men. The text certainly makes clear that whatever they say, their faces readily betray their inner emotions. Marwood turns red at Mrs Fainall's 'Ingenious mischief! Would thou wert married to Mirabell', and then Mrs Fainall, when she defends Mirabell against the accusation of being proud, both flushes and turns pale. (She pretends it is because her husband has entered, but since Mirabell arrives with him, no one will credit *that* explanation.) The women's more overt sexual passions, then, put them at a disadvantage, and to reveal one's emotions involuntarily is dangerous in this kind of world, as will be seen when Mr Fainall reduces Marwood to tears. Lady Wishfort we shall also perceive exposed *in extremis*. Only Millamant manages to hide her feelings behind a smokescreen of verbal badinage, but that affectation makes her almost a fool and a companion of Witwoud and Petulant.

The subsequent scene between Mr Fainall and Marwood in which she breaks down is bleak and cruel. The viciousness of the man's character and the wayward lust of the woman eventually erupt through the veneer of manners; the verbal fencing of earlier exchanges now becomes bloody in purpose, and reaches its logical conclusion in physical violence. Consider, initially, Mr Fainall's words as his wife leaves him and Marwood together, being more eager to enjoy the company of her (former?) lover than concerned at leaving her husband alone with his mistress: 'Excellent creature! Well, sure, if I should live to be rid of my wife, I should be a miserable man.' The paradox he intends is witty: if she died or were divorced he would lose his 'one hope', to be free of her, and what is life without hope? Obliquely, however, he is also attacking Marwood as well as Mrs Fainall. He certainly does not want Marwood as a new wife, and does not count her among his 'hopes'. It is an elegantly tangential way of informing her he no longer has any interest in their relationship. She is left almost speechless. The tone of her mere 'Aye!' is indefinable – it takes the rest of the episode to elucidate why she agrees – and then her words 'Will you not follow 'em?' are highly ambiguous. Has she been so hurt by his sarcasm that she will gladly surrender this opportunity to be alone with her lover? Or is it that her desire for Mirabell has totally distracted her from Mr Fainall? If so, her own sexually motivated eagerness that her lover should be gone is as insulting to Mr Fainall as his own innuendo was to her: that he has no hopes which involve her. The tensions between them are so complex that it is the

husband (Mr Fainall) who accuses his mistress (Marwood) of being
jealous of his wife's companion (Mirabell – Mr Fainall is unaware
Mirabell has been Mrs Fainall's lover). Conventional morality would be
that it is the husband who should be jealous that his wife is in the
company of another man.

It is frequently the case in this play that, in exchanges of this kind, the
innuendos are more important than the superficial moral sentiments,
which are, in any case, often questionable in the abstract, and in context:
for instance Marwood's 'is it inconsistent with my love to you that I am
tender of your honour?' Like 'friendship' throughout the play, the
words 'love' and 'honour' here are counterfeit. For the first understand
'lust', for the second something like 'face' or 'reputation'. A rake can
have no true honour or love. Marwood's point is merely that it will do
Mr Fainall's reputation no good to become a subject of scandal and ridicule because his wife has cuckolded him – but she lies anyway, trying to
conceal her passion for Mirabell.

In this looking-glass world, the husband 'fears' Mirabell is 'insensible'
to his wife (because if she had an affair he might pursue his own more
easily?), and the word 'deceived' is switched from the cuckolder
(Mirabell) to the husband's mistress (Marwood): 'I have been deceived,
madam, and you are false.' Mr Fainall does not care sexually what his
wife does, but he is concerned about what his mistress feels: 'could you
think, because the nodding husband would not wake, that e'er the
watchful lover slept?' This opposition between 'husband' and 'lover' is
central to the libertine ethos of much Restoration comedy with the
implication that sexual gratification exists only outside marriage. That
Mr Fainall should, at this juncture, both be jealous of his mistress, and
dislike her also, is only too clear a manifestation of that 'unhappy circumstance of life' ennunciated as being the common condition of women at
the beginning of the act.

Once again Marwood's emotions betray her. Mr Fainall has noted her
red cheeks and sparkling eyes. Her proclamation, delivered with feeling,
that she 'hates' Mirabell only confirms, on the contrary, the depth of her
sexual desire for him. She is exposed, therefore, and any person in this
world who lays themselves open in this way is vulnerable to malice,
scandal and ridicule. We have seen this sportively attempted by Witwoud and Petulant, while Mirabell, on Mrs Fainall's testimony, call tell a
good tale this way, now we see the real thing as Mr Fainall performs

execution. Marwood, of course, throws off the customary cloud of moral evasions like a cuttle-fish emitting black ink, but there is no need to examine the casuistry of her talk about 'professed friendship', 'fidelity', 'love inviolate', 'merit' and so on. The man goes straight to the heart of the hypocrisy of the matter: 'Professed a friendship! Oh, the pious friend-ships of the female sex!' and then 'Ha! ha! ha! you are my wife's friend too'. The word 'professed' is twisted to mean 'tell a lie'; 'friendship' is turned inside out. The tone is scornful, the intention is deliberately malicious. Marwood states so directly. She is simply being held up to ridicule, and Mr Fainall abandons all the potential misrepresentations of words: he need do no more than laugh at her to drive her to 'frenzy'.

It is the second time we have heard laughter on stage in this act. The previous occasion was Marwood taunting Mrs Fainall for being confused at the arrival of Mirabell. The biter is now bit, and for the same cause. Whatever Marwood 'professes' to Lady Wishfort or Mrs Fainall as a 'friend' or to Mr Fainall as a mistress, she cannot conceal her frustrated passion. The laughter in both cases is an instrument of ridicule, close to that 'malicious pleasure' which Dryden detected as a basis of mirth.[7] It is not only without heart, but here it is not even the purgative ridicule of wholesome satire. The one motive is to inflict pain.

How much Mr Fainall himself is emotionally hurt by the infidelity of his mistress we have no means of telling. Presumably his pride is damaged, but his words give nothing away. More manifest is the fact that his pocket has been threatened because of Marwood's jealous revela-tion through 'professed friendship' to Lady Wishfort that Mirabell's approaches to the old lady are a dissimulatory blind for courtship of Millamant. This relevation has potentially come between Mr Fainall and the money he will get if Millamant marries without her aunt's (Lady Wishfort's) permission. Presumably this is why he chooses to cut Marwood to ribbons on this issue. The matter is complex considered merely at the level of plot, but the emotional development of the scene is more complex yet.

Mr Fainall's laughter has gone too far. Marwood has been goaded beyond endurance. Once the rules of the game of professed friendship, honour and fidelity are broken, scandal must be the result, and, for Mr Fainall, financial disaster also at his wife's hands if his promiscuity is revealed. Marwood, determined to strike back at any cost, cries (concern-ing the whole situation):

It shall be all discovered. You too shall be discovered; be sure you shall. I can but be exposed. If I do it myself, I shall prevent your baseness.

Probably Mr Fainall had realized as soon as he had laughed at her that he had gone too far, for his next speeches show him striving to moderate the position, while Marwood progressively becomes angrier. The psychological nicety of this is admirable. So convincing is the progression of the quarrel that we may hypothesize more than one latent motive for the woman's rage. Ridiculed by her lover (Mr Fainall); and rejected by the man she wants (Mirabell), she is sexually so humiliated that a public outburst would be a relief for her repressed passions. Furthermore, to provoke a quarrel with Mr Fainall would be one way of ending a stale affair. At the end of such relationships people look for a *casus belli*. When both are tense and involved in dishonesty, such provocation is never difficult to find.

From Mr Fainall's point of view, however, public scandal is 'frenzy'. He has the colder, more calculating mind, and although he has just as much a wish to quarrel as she, faced with the possible consequences, he has the commonsense to observe that Marwood must be stopped. The only way to do this is to keep the affair – which is dead – alive. The punishment of the man who has deceived his wife to win a mistress, is that to retain his wife he must continue the deceit with the mistress whom he no longer desires, and who herself wants another.

He returns, accordingly, to the language of a rake's courtship: 'wherefore did I marry, but to make lawful prize of a rich widow's wealth, and to squander it on love and you?' . . . 'Will you yet be reconciled to truth and me?' . . . 'You know I love you'. The words 'love' and 'truth' carry no conviction either for the audience or Marwood. Her determination to part from him, and his own alarm (*not* loving concern): 'Nay, we must not part thus', leads to the physical climax of the episode in which Mr Fainall has to use the superior strength of masculine mastery to force Marwood to remain.

At this point Marwood's natural psychological progression through frustration is to inarticulateness and tears. Ultimately she knows as well as he that public scandal is outside the rules of the game, and that they are therefore stuck with one another almost as much as if they were married.

Fainall   You know I love you.

Mrs Marwood   Poor dissembling! Oh, that — Well, it is not yet —
Fainall   What? what is not? What is it not yet? It is not yet too late —
Mrs Marwood   No, it is not yet too late; I have that comfort.
Fainall   It is, to love another.
Mrs Marwood   But not to loathe, detest, abhor mankind, myself and the whole treacherous world.
Fainall   Nay, this is extravagance. Come, I ask your pardon. No tears. I was to blame; I could not love you and be easy in my doubts. Pray, forbear. I believe you. I'm convinced I've done you wrong; and any way, every way will make amends. I'll hate my wife yet more, damn her! I'll part with her, rob her of all she's worth, and we'll retire somewhere, anywhere, to another world. I'll marry thee; be pacified. 'Sdeath, they come; hide your face, your tears. You have a mask; wear it a moment. This way, this way, Be persuaded.

Exeunt

The discrepancy between the psychological situation and the words spoken here is extreme. It is impossible to finish Marwood's unconcluded sentence with confidence: 'Oh, that — Well, it is not yet — '. Does 'that' refer to 'dissembling'; or 'love', or has she begun an optative expression: would that such and such were true, or might happen? Is Mr Fainall's expansion of 'it is not yet' with the words 'too late' correct? If it is, is her spoken conclusion what was originally in her mind? It is not yet too late to part with Mr Fainall, to give herself to Mirabell, to reveal Mr Fainall as her lover. These are all obvious continuations. These verbal developments, however, do not correspond with what seems feasible. They are like King Lear's proclamation in rage that he will do such things — but what they are he knows not. Such frustration naturally leads to a non-verbal outlet in hysteria and tears, and the extravagance of her utterance that she hates herself, all men, 'and the whole treacherous world'. The 'unhappy circumstance' of woman's role as man's prey, which seemed mere cynical rhetoric at the beginning of the act, is once more reinforced.

    The text indicates that she yields, up to a point, to Mr Fainall's blandishments as she weeps. He takes physical charge of her bodily movements, but she would be a fool to believe what he says to her. The growing 'extravagance' of his own speech is evidence of hypocrisy as he urgently seeks to get her to control herself before Mirabell and Mrs

Fainall return. The promise that he will rob his wife is manifest nonsense — though any financially crippled divorcee will recognize the desire — and at the end of the play he is driven to the point of wishing to kill Mrs Fainall to recover financial control of his own destiny. The words 'we'll retire somewhere, anywhere, to another world' are equally preposterous, and will be thematically redeveloped at the end of the play when the harrassed Lady Wishfort cries to her 'friend' Marwood 'let us leave the world, and retire by ourselves and be shepherdesses.' There is, of course, no other world but the ways of this present 'treacherous' one. Such romanticism is folly. Lady Wishfort accordingly totters into comic absurdity with the vision of herself minding sheep, and Mr Fainall himself reaches an equally absurd climactic utterance: 'I'll marry thee' — a lie, forced out of him in desperation to offer Marwood anything to keep her quiet. If the absurdity of this utterance moves the audience to laughter, it is the sardonic mockery of those who recognize the evils of wedlock. Marwood's own views on the married condition (if they are honest) have recently been given to the suffering Mrs Fainall. Matrimony is a state she desires because of the exquisite power it gives to hurt the man one hates. At the point when Mr Fainall (falsely) proposes to her, she puts on her mask to conceal her tears. It is a physical icon for most of what has passed in the play so far. All are deceivers. But a more treacherous deceiver than herself leads her by the hand. For Mr Fainall, his own face is sufficient mask.

This is the cue for the return of the more successful deceiving couple: Mirabell and Mrs Fainall. As so often in the early scenes of this play it is a matter of some niceness to distinguish between hero and villain. It is a point in Mirabell's favour that he and his mistress do not quarrel and that they have been able to suspend their affair (it seems) and maintain a friendship free from rancour and ridicule. They are able to trust one another with confidences. Mirabell has charm and grace which wins the heart of all women. Yet, when that is granted, the content of what is said between the new couple closely relates to what has passed between Mr Fainall and Marwood. Mrs Fainall (like Marwood) betrays a potentially dangerous emotion in her statement that, since she grew from hating to despising her husband, he is too offensive to see. If there is to be the scandal of a separation, what embarrassing factors may be revealed? Mirabell, (like Mr Fainall) therefore counsels against extravagance: 'Oh, you should hate with prudence'. His next speech might with equal propriety be given to the villain for it is a straight libertine utterance (and which may imply a future continuance of their affair):

> You should have just so much disgust for your husband as may be sufficient to make you relish your lover.

This masculine coolness, however, is threatened by the woman's emotionalism. 'You have been the cause that I have loved without bounds', and one detects genuine feeling and pain behind Mrs Fainall's: 'Why did you make me marry this man?' Mirabell's explanation is a major problem. Just as much as Mr Fainall he is concerned with 'that idol, reputation'. It is the essential rule of the sexual game played by the 'treacherous world' that reputation must be preserved. Husbands and wives, while hating and deceiving one another, must maintain their honour by appearing faithful in public; the unmarried promiscuously couple, yet the woman, at least, must seem to be chaste. This is the mask of 'profession' which everyone wears. Hence the need to provide a husband for Mrs Fainall when Mirabell thought she was pregnant by him. Mr Fainall lied to Marwood when he said 'I'll marry thee'; Mirabell, on the other hand, never contemplated such a foolish possibility as wedding his mistress. Yet, however much one may seek to admire the ingenuity of his calculation that Mr Fainall was the right man to be palmed off with a bastard, the characterization of the husband chosen for Mirabell's mistress only too clearly provides ground for Mrs Fainall's pain and complaint: 'a man lavish of his morals, an interested and professing friend, a false and a designing lover'. The problem is, change places, and that description equally well fits Mirabell. The explanation ends with the most notorious ambiguity of the play, Mirabell's statement, 'When you are weary of him, you know your remedy.' Presumably, in the light of information we discover in the fifth act, Mirabell refers to the deed in the black box which will give Mrs Fainall independence from her husband. No member of the audience can know this now, however, and the remedy which will spring to mind is very different. It sounds like an offer to recommence their affair.

Should one view Mirabell at this juncture as honest – at least with his mistress – ? Pretend as we will, the world is really like this. Or should one join with Jeremy Collier, and all those since, who feel morally outraged by Congreve? Perhaps Congreve was telling the truth when he answered Collier's censures by arguing that his plays were satirical, and, thus, even his hero will not escape censure? These are challenging issues for they involve the deepest values of our own sexual morality and pass beyond the confines of expository literary criticism. It is necessary to give a literary context to these matters, however, by asking a simple question: what degree of naturalism is one to assume in this plot? How much of what is happening on stage is supposed to reflect the world as it really was, or is generically determined, rather, by the provocatively libertine conventions of Restoration comic form?

This exposition so far has treated character in action naturalistically. The justification for an approach to the play as if it concerned real people is that only in this way can situation, motive, and dialogue be understood. The men and women of this play will frequently imply what they do not say, mean something else than what they declare, and their emotional progression has a development beneath the text, bending it in unexpected directions, provoking developments or jumps which can only be explained by imagining what would be going on inside the personages if they were truly alive. Congreve has been considered as if he were Chekhov. The psychological methods of Stanislavski would be appropriate for the players creating the roles.

This approach must now be qualified. Because this is comedy, generic conventions will apply. Marwood's passion, for example, will not produce a tragic catastrophe; hero and heroine will be rewarded in a happy marriage – however unhappy other marriages are shown to be; vice will be punished but not too severely. The elements of generic control are tighter than that, however, because of the local development of motifs by the 'Restoration' mutation of comic form. Certain characters, situations, attitudes are conventional stock-in-trade at this time. They are so standardized that minor works of the kind are monotonously predictable (compare television sit. com.), and, superficially considered, even the major products of this dramatic school have a strong familiar relationship. Rake, cuckold, cast mistress, for instance, are conventional roles. Mirabell, Mr Fainall and Mrs Fainall, conform, in general, to stage types. (This is generally true of all the characters within the play.)

The paradox, then, is that although the speech of a character such as Mirabell must frequently be read naturalistically to be understood, the kind of character he is has been conventionally determined by innumerable other comedies, and the situations in which he acts often have no credible existence except in the theatre. This is obvious in the latter half of

Mirabell's dialogue with Mrs Fainall when he explains the plot to pass Waitwell off as Sir Rowland in order to deceive Lady Wishfort into a bogus marriage and secure Millamant's fortune by subsequent blackmail. It would be absurd to discuss such a strategm in terms of the morality of the real world, for such a device is preposterous outside comic theatre. The function of this device is to bring about the happy ending of the play: the hero wins the heroine and her money, and Lady Wishfort is correctively purged of her foolish amorous lusts (if only temporarily). Thus the device which naturalistically conceived would be morally dubious (were it even possible) and potentially illegal – and hence is 'bad' – nonetheless within the comic play would bring about the desired resolution – and hence is 'good'.

Mirabell's marrying off his cast mistress to Mr Fainall must be considered likewise in relation to theatrical convention and function. It is merely a comic device like the Sir Rowland plot. This is not to deny that the naturalistic conviction of some of the writing makes us consider actors morally as if they were real. The effect of this is to introduce an element of tension between different strands in the play – let us call them generic modes – which deny simple categorization. It is a matter readily enough recognized in Shakespearian theatre which moves, for instance, quickly between verisimilitude and allegory, psychological truth and choric utterance. The changes are not always so obvious in Congreve because of a greater stylistic uniformity, but the superficial appearance of naturalism behind the polished manners of a recognizable social world should not be allowed to obliterate distinctions between modes.

This is not to proffer an answer to the old question of the relation of art to life, nor even to defend the sexual morality of Restoration comedy. But there is a difference between debating as a real issue the question should a man marry his mistress to another if he thinks she is pregnant? and the matter as it is raised between characters whose being and action and determined by the conventions of comic theatre in the late seventeenth century. More informative, therefore, than a casuistical discussion upon morality is an understanding of how Congreve adapts those conventions in portraying Mirabell. To pursue even this to its last ramifications would be a large issue for it involves the whole relation of the hero as rake and/or romantic lover in the comedy of the time. A specific (and notorious) instance must suffice, therefore, to illustrate the point.

Compare Dorimant in Etherege's *The Man of Mode* (1676). This play is so full of suggestions of *The Way of the World* that one may hazard the speculation that Congreve was consciously reworking the earlier dramatist's motifs. Both heroes have the promiscuous sexual confidence which had received classic formulation in Jonson's characterization by Truewit:

> A man should not doubt to overcome any woman. Think he can vanquish them, and he shall: for though they deny, their desire is to be tempted. Penelope herself cannot hold out long.[8]

Both also have witchcraft in word and manner − so Lady Woodvill in Etherege: 'Oh, he has a tongue, they say, would tempt the angels to a second fall' (III. iii, 115 – 16)[9] and Lady Wishfort in Congreve: 'Oh, he has witchcraft in his eyes and tongue' (V.378). Dorimant and Mirabell have the graces of literary learning; both are similarly disturbed at finding themselves in love with a chaste woman who is their mental match − *Dorimant:* 'I love her and dare not let her know it' (IV. i. 139); and both, with a keen eye to financial settlement, are forced to contemplate marriage in a world where wedlock is generally held in ill-repute: 'We speak to one another civilly, hate one another heartily, and because 'tis vulgar to lie and soak together, we have each of us our several . . . bed'[10] (I. i. 284 – 6).

Dorimant, however, calculatingly pursues an affair with one woman (Bellinda) even while courting Harriet whom he truly loves, whereas Mirabell, on the contrary, rejects Marwood, and his relation with Lady Wishfort is merely a flirtation designed to win access to Millamant. Etherege's hero treats his cast mistress (Loveit) with a deliberate (and competitive) cruelty, utterly at variance with Mirabell's subtler and politer dealing with Mrs Fainall which sustains her affection even while he uses (and protects) her. There is, above all, an instability about Dorimant and a coarseness in his view of sexual relations, which ultimately betrays him, provoking the surprise ending where Harriet refuses to risk herself in marriage (at least at this juncture). Millamant, though having very good reason to fear Mirabell, is wooed by him with honest respect and love, and is won by a man who convinces her that he will be a good husband and *not* in the way of the world. If Dorimant is taken as normative of the rakish hero of Restoration comedy, then, in comparison, Mirabell is a reformed man. Or, put another way, the Fainall/Marwood imbroglio reveals what the selfish promiscuity of the rake may lead to, while, in contrast, the marriage of Mirabell with Millamant indicates a pathway – however tortuous – to as much happiness and stability as this world may offer.

Such comparative morality may not satisfy those of purer heart, and the contrast of one aspect of a mutating theatrical genre with another may be no more than an aesthetic evasion. Nonetheless, in the play world, Mirabell proves a more successful and happier man than Dorimant, and, if one wishes to make the distinction, is he not a better man also?

3. *The heroine: II. 291 – 451*

It can do Millamant's reputation no good to arrive in the company of Witwoud. He is not the kind of man a sensible woman would allow to court her favours, or (to consider the matter in terms of generic convention), being paired off with him as Petulant was earlier, places the heroine among the play's fools. Indeed, it appears that Millamant has chosen that role for herself. She plays the fool so brilliantly and so consistently that it is often difficult to intuit what (if anything) is behind the facade of breathless affectation.

If we compare her initial dialogue either with the strongly naturalistic portrayal of Mrs Marwood, or with what is revealed by Mrs Fainall's cry, 'Why did you make me marry this man?' she will appear emotionally thin. In fact she is a practised hypocrite, like Mirabell, and more successfully than the other women of the play finds, in the torrent of her badinage, a disguise for her feelings. What those feelings may be is not initially apparent. Since this is the 'heroine', romantic convention demands emotional commitment to the 'hero'. But we will only glimpse this momentarily later. The audience have to follow the game according to the order in which Congreve lays down the cards, and Millamant appears at first no more than a character of affectation:

> Here she comes, i' faith, full sail, with her fan spread and her streamers out, and a shoal of fools for tenders.

The preposterous, of course, is tempered by sexual charm. As Colley Cibber noted of Anne Bracegirdle, the original creator of the role: 'all the faults, follies, and affectations of that agreeable tyrant were venially melted down into so many charms and attractions of a conscious beauty.'[11] That seems the right kind of combination for the actress, but the terms 'folly', 'affectation' and even 'tyranny' must be given their proper weight.

The word 'affectation' had an especial significance for Congreve. In his letter *Concerning Humour in Comedy* to the critic John Dennis he describes it not only as one of the prime sources of comedy, but also as a particular characteristic of women. The distinction made there is between a true 'humour' which is 'A singular and unavoidable manner of doing, or saying any thing, Peculiar and Natural to one Man only' and in its origin psychological or pathological; and on the other hand, 'affectation' which is the pretence of being what one is not. The braggart soldier (*miles gloriosus*) always seeking a quarrel, but who never saw battle and is a coward at heart, is a typical example Congreve offers of affectation. Petulant, in this play, is a lateral branch of that species. The very name of his companion Witwoud formally places that character as another unnatural pretender — the lad from the Wrekin who sets up as a man of mode.

The origin of these ideas is in the plays of Ben Jonson (though it is Congrevian cynicism to suggest that women are both too cold and too passionate to have true 'humour'). Given these theories, it is a peculiar piece of daring to establish Millamant formally in the camp of the ridiculous. It is reminiscent of pairing the hero with the villain. The heroine is so close to the fools with whom she associates that not only is niceness of distinction required to separate her attitudes from theirs, but at times her function in the comedy is indistinguishable.

One use of Petulant and Witwoud by the dramatist is to satirize the false manners of society by showing absurd excess: witness Petulant's attempt to appear a rake by having whores call for him, or even calling for himself, (unless that is Witwoud's malicious invention). Millamant's first burst of affectation is similar in its sexual vanity. Consider her on the multiplicity of her lovers represented by the *billets doux* with which she claims she is troubled:

> Oh, aye, letters; I had letters. I am persecuted with letters. I hate letters. Nobody knows how to write letters; and yet one has 'em, one does not know why. They serve one to pin up one's hair . . . Only with those in verse, Mr Witwoud. I never pin up my hair with prose. I fancy one's hair would not curl if it were pinned up with prose. I think I tried once, Mincing.

Millamant's affectation is suggested by her name just as much as Petulant's and Witwoud's. She claims that she makes lovers as fast as she pleases, and cares for none of them. They serve only to flatter her pride, as their letters serve to enhance the (extravagant?) artificiality of the curls of her hair. It is delightful prattle, but it does not serve to recommend her as a wife.

How is this to be distinguished from Petulant's or Witwoud's folly? The most obvious thing, though indefinable, is that she is much funnier, and that she compels the audience to laugh *with* her at her image of herself, whereas our laughter is directed (for instance) *at* Witwoud at this juncture with his train of inappropriate similitudes. Whether she really made the experiment with the letters must remain among the play's ambiguities. Probably she has launched into a realm of delicious fantasy (backed up by Mincing) so far-fetched that she does not expect an intelligent man like Mirabell to believe her, but, rather, to admire her ridiculous rhapsody. The difference between this and Petulant's whores in a coach, or Lady Wishfort rouging herself for a lover later, is that these fools hope to deceive by their affectations, whereas Millamant might claim to be following the Horatian dictum: *dulce est dissipere in loco*. Even the wise like to play the fool on the right occasion, a sentiment which Socrates and Sir Thomas More would share. Finally, one must take into account generic expectation. The kind of badinage which Millamant provokes may be traced back at least as far as Shakespeare's Beatrice. Thence, via Beaumont and Fletcher and James Shirley, the tradition had descended to the Restoration of merry lovers who conceal their affection behind wit and flippancy. One may find Millamant's type everywhere in the comedy of the age.[12]

Nevertheless even Mirabell was led to catalogue Millamant's faults, and her kind of affected prattle, however charming, is a cause of unease. It is very risky for a woman, in a malicious and censorious world, to make herself the butt of laughter even if she expects to be admired for it. Witwoud shows a similar complacent pride: 'I confess I do blaze today; I am too bright.' If Millamant is pleased with her ability to make lovers like *him* as fast as she pleases, it is no wonder she is persecuted with letters only fit to pin up her hair. Her pretended silliness begets all too easily real stupidity.

If she is to satisfy the audience as a proper match for Mirabell, Congreve must reveal, behind her delicious mask of affectation, not only real feeling, but also the necessary sharpness, and even hardness to survive the ways of the world. It is not always easy to demonstrate this initially from the text, but at least the question may be put, how much more knowing is Millamant than she seems, even at her seemingly most naive? Consider the following fragment of dialogue:

Millamant   (to Mrs Fainall) I have asked every living thing I met for you; I have inquired after you, as after a new fashion.

Witwoud Madam, truce with your similitudes. No, you met her husband, and did not ask him for her.
Mirabell By your leave, Witwoud, that were like inquiring after an old fashion, to ask a husband for his wife.

It seems routine enough. But has Millamant been betrayed inadvertantly into a 'similitude', or has she consciously directed it at Witwoud, mocking his patter? Witwoud, claims he has caught her out, whereas he is caught, and Mirabell, instantly spotting what Millamant is about, caps her wit with yet another similitude. This ability of the lovers to read the other's mind without direct communication and reciprocate intelligently is highly important, especially, as we shall see, during the proposal and proviso scenes. Further, has Millamant foolishly forgotten she met Mr Fainall and prattles nonsense − as Witwoud thinks − or has she shown by not asking the husband where his wife is, that she is fully aware that the question is inappropriate for him? She knows what state that marriage is in. Possibly this interpretation over-reads Millamant's acuteness, but there can be no doubt of it at the end of the episode. She saves up her revelation that she knows the Sir Rowland plot until just the moment to halt Mirabell in his tracks with her off-hand revelation. It lets her lover know she is on a par with him in Machiavellian intelligence.

Behind the coquette there is a needle-sharp woman. It would be inappropriate to sentimentalize her, though her charm and her looks are among her weapons. She uses both her attractiveness and her wit to give pain if need be. She states that this pleases her 'infinitely': 'I love to give pain.' Mirabell, using the *précieux* vocabulary of courtly love, claims that his 'cruelty' is yet another of her affectations, but he is a biased witness. When Millamant is confronted with Marwood later there is no doubt that she enjoys hurting the older woman. That Marwood deserves it may make the cruelty just, but it is there nonetheless. The comic tradition in which Congreve is writing derives from Jonson, and *Epicoene* was in his mind when he wrote this play. Truewit there (whom Congreve admired) goes out of his way to invent humiliating torments for the humourists and fools whose company he seeks out to amuse him. Millamant is not as malicious as that, but it is an 'unfortunate circumstance' that one needs to be armed and to be hard to survive the ways of this world.

The reasons why Millamant masks her feelings behind affectation, and wounds when she has need, derive from sexual vulnerability, emotionally and financially. It is typical of the play's obliqueness that this should be

most clearly revealed by Millamant's reading of Sir John Suckling and
this will be considered in its place later. Meantime, her explanation of her
cruelty touches the hard centre of the comedy:

> One's cruelty is one's power; and when one parts with one's cruelty,
> one parts with one's power; and when one has parted with that, I
> fancy one's old and ugly.

The kind of world she envisages is not unlike the state of nature as
described by her contemporary, the philosopher Hobbes. It is a state of
war of each against each. To survive, therefore, one needs some sort of
weapon, for those who do not have power over others will be subservient
to them. The rules of this war in civilized society are artificial, but the
struggle is fierce. A young woman has one major card she can play: her
sexuality, but nature has put a date on that, and the rules of society insist
that usually she can only play that card once with propriety. She may
choose a husband, but once married, power has passed into his hands. A
Halifax observed in his *Advice to a Daughter* (1688):

> the laws of marriage run in a harsher style towards your sex [than for a
> man]. Obey is an ungenteel word, and less easy to be digested by
> making such an unkind distinction in the words of the contract.[13]

Hence the importance of the proviso scene between Mirabell and
Millamant. Whatever the demands of the marriage ceremony that the
woman obey, theirs is to be a contract negotiated between equals.

Another source of power would be money. But half Millamant's
fortune depends upon her marrying with her aunt's consent. She is not
free to play her hand, therefore, as she would wish. Millamant must
accordingly consider both the emotional risk in giving her love, and the
financial consequences. It is part of the test of the suitability of Mirabell to
be her husband that he has sufficient cunning to get both her, and all her
fortune. In the real world a John Churchill might marry just for love, and
entail a lifetime of notorious meanness upon himself. In romantic comedy
like *Love for Love* a profligate, spendthrift Valentine might win an
Angelica and her wealth, by showing he cares nothing for money without
out her. In the ways of the world of this play, however, the importance
of wealth is never denied. Lovers who destroy their financial integrity to
satisfy sexual desire are fools. That is why when Mirabell married his cast
mistress to Mr Fainall he secured her financial independence at the same

time but subject to his own control. It was a vital step. Without it his
plot would collapse at the end of the play. With the money Mrs Fainall
has the power to control her husband.

Hence too the uneasiness of an earlier remark of Mirabell's to Mrs
Fainall:

> In justice to you, I have made you privy to my whole design, and put
> it in your power to ruin or advance my fortune.

What he is forced to rely on here is precisely the same power that
Millamant exercises over him: youthful sexuality. Nor may one deny his
cruelty to Mrs Fainall. Having taken her body, thereafter he uses her as he
needs. Paradoxically, it is by denying herself sexually that Millamant is
able to exert power over Mirabell. There are complex emotional reasons
underlying her feeling that she needs power, but there is a material necessity also. She not only wants Mirabell on her own terms, she wants him
to get her money for her.

One final example of the interrelation of sexuality with power is
Mirabell's attitude to Waitwell and Foible. Why marry them off before
using Waitwell as Sir Rowland to obtain power over Lady Wishfort?
The answer is spelled out in the hard terms of Jonsonian theatre:

> I would not tempt my servant to betray me by trusting him too far. If
> [Lady Wishfort] . . . in hopes to ruin me, should consent to marry
> my pretended uncle, he might, like Mosca in *The Fox*, stand upon
> terms; so I made him sure beforehand.

No one trusts anybody unless they are sure they have a hold on them first.
This applies to Millamant's view of Mirabell just as much as his attitude
to his own servant.

These are unattractive sentiments. When glossed in this manner they
have lost the grace and wit of their comic expression, and, on the page,
they have lost also the ineffable charm of youthful sexuality with which
the players of Mirabell and Millamant will invest them in their love
debate. It would be misleading, therefore, for this analysis to become too
solemn and fail to acknowledge the inspiriting elements of fantasy and
game which are everywhere in the dialogue:

> Why, one makes lovers as fast as one pleases, and they live as long as
> one pleases, and they die as soon as one pleases; and then, if one
> pleases, one makes more.

This is 'very pretty' — as Witwoud observes, and exposition of this swift-footed banter must always seem pedantic and heavy. The lovers are sexually enjoying the stimulation of a *précieux débat*: is beauty the lover's gift, or does beauty make the lover? Yet the comedy would be vapid if it did not turn to laughter what are serious, and even unpleasant, issues when seen from an alternative viewpoint. Sex is cruel. There is a struggle for power between men and women. To adopt Byron's observation: if we laugh at anything, it is because we would not weep.

In the debate, it is the ridiculous Millamant who turns the tables on Mirabell by placing him in the absurd position of someone seeking to be earnest in a comedy. When he asks her to be serious for a moment, she exclaims:

> What, with that face? No, if you keep your countenance,
> 'tis impossible I should hold mine.

One might expect — now the couple are alone — Millamant to drop her defensive affectation and show the sincerity of her feelings (and they *are* sincere). Yet she sustains a barrage of mockery against which the man is helpless, because he has betrayed himself as manifestly in love, and hence he is in her power:

> *Millamant* Ha! ha! ha! What would you give that you could help loving me?
> *Mirabell* I would give something that you did not know I could not help it.

Ridicule is the source of the self-congratulatory delight of laughter here, as with Marwood's mockery of Mrs Fainall, and Mr Fainall's of Marwood. If Millamant's is sympathetic teasing — happy lovers like to laugh at one another sometimes — it still maintains something of the salt relish of cruelty.

What is being mocked is the attempt by Mirabell to assume the role of a man of sincerity, a 'plain dealer' to adopt an expression from Wycherley's comedy, or — if one prefers the French phrase — *un honnête homme*, whose *honnêté* includes the meanings of integrity, propriety, fair dealing, and civility. One may find general parallels in Molière, or (later) in the humane comedies of Richard Steele. Generally, or psychologically, considered, the Machiavellian Mirabell is seeking to become a lover whose virtues are frankness and good sense. Along with Millamant he assumes the prerogatives one might almost claim of a husband rather than a lover and reproves her for the blatant affectation of her pleasure in the company of Petulant and Witwoud: 'How can you find delight in such society? . . . to please a fool is some degree of folly.' Since he wants to broach the subject of marriage he seeks to restrain the 'whirlwind', the 'windmill', and win her 'with plain dealing and sincerity'. Millamant's refusal to restrain the 'variety' of her disposition to let him get a word in is among the funniest sequences of the play. Yet the justness of Mirabell's complaint on the mobility of women should not be neglected:

> motion, not method, is their occupation. To know this, and yet
> continue to be in love, is to be made wise from the dictates
> of reason, and yet persevere to play the fool by the force of instinct.

Mirabell's error is one of tact. The man of wit and pleasure has begun to sound too like a nagging husband – Millamant complains 'I shan't endure to be reprimanded nor instructed; 'tis so dull to act always by advice, and so tedious to be hold of one's faults.'[14] The literal application of those sentiments would merely serve to confirm a fool in her folly, but the implications of her sub-text are probably Horatian once again: *Ridentem dicere verum quid vetat?* One should make moral truth attractive by making it amusing, which is what the plain dealer fails to do. There is a long tradition in satiric comedy that any character who sets himself up as a wise man on this great stage of fools runs the risk of appearing grotesquely puritanical: 'Dost thou think because thou art virtuous there shall be no more cakes and ale?' Sir Toby Belch asked Malvolio. A long line of Surlys, Moroses, Aspers, Overdos, had been created by Jonson. All are made to stand as butts for ridicule rather than being straight-forward honest satirists, and Mirabell, peevish, with a violent, inflexible, wise face 'like Solomon at the dividing of the child' runs the risk of joining that type. After all, like Angelo, he is in no position to lay down the law about proper behaviour. It is when he meets Millamant later on the same level of high fantasy on which she lives, and trades wit for wit, that by sexual grace and comic laughter he negotiates the famous provisos for their future married life, and wins her hand. Just as honesty will not win a fortune in this world, plain dealing is not enough to entice, win and keep a happy wife.

4. *The proposal of marriage: IV. 60 – 289*

The proposal of marriage never deviates into sentimentality. It is always witty, but the comedy is a fragile bridge over an abyss of staleness, promiscuity and unhappiness.

The episode is prepared by Sir Wilfull's abortive courtship of Millamant which, in the business of the locked door, approaches farce. Like the heroine, here we enjoy her diet of fools. At the same time, the contrast between this wooer, and Mirabell who succeeds him, resolves Millamant's mind. There is a further element in the prolegomena. Sir Wilfull is diversely used by Congreve. Although he is a natural unsophisticate, like Sailor Ben in *Love for Love*, he is also used to ridicule the affectations of artificial society: witness the scene in which Petulant and Witwoud set out to 'smoke' him and are smoked instead. Likewise, the satire in the courtship sequence is not all directed at him, even though he is fuddled with drink, for Millamant is in one of her perverse, 'windmill' moods. 'I nauseate walking; 'tis a country diversion. I loathe the country and everything that relates to it . . . Ah, *l'étourdie!* I hate the town too.' If Sir Wilfull is an anti-type of a noble savage, Millamant here scarcely represents the finest aspect of high civilization. An affectation for French phrases is a common source of ridicule in Restoration comedy (cf. Dryden's *Marriage à la Mode*), and the person who can live neither in the town nor the country is a common butt of satire from Horace to Pope.

Moreover, though Millamant's laughter at her cousin is shared with the audience, she is unable to deal with him in any polite or even practical way. One notices that even Lady Wishfort socially was able to put Sir Wilfull in the way of *politesse* on his arrival, and confronted with him drunk later, she has the robust commonsense necessary to handle the problem, whereas Millamant merely beats a hasty retreat. Who has the worse of the following exchange?

Millamant (*repeating*). I swear it will not do its part,
Though thou dost thine, employ'st thy power and art.
Natural, easy Suckling!

Sir Wilfull   Anan? Suckling? No such suckling neither, cousin, nor stripling; I thank heaven, I'm no minor.
Millamant   Ah, rustic! ruder than Gothic!
Sir Wilfull   Well, well, I shall understand your lingo one of these days, cousin; in the meanwhile, I must answer in plain English.

Sir Wilfull shows a deplorable (perhaps) want of knowledge of the niceties of polite literature, for he has not heard of a minor cavalier poet some fifty years *passé*, but is not the young woman rudely showing off? The balance of sympathy in the laughter is necessary, for Congreve must later use Sir Wilfull as a 'good' character at the play's resolution.

Millamant's taste for Sir John Suckling (1609 – 42) must be further considered. The verses, which have been running in her head all day, (Mrs Fainall tells us) are an indication of the furniture of her mind, and a clear clue to the brittleness of her attitude to men and marriage. She describes the poet not only as natural and easy, but as 'filthy' also. The poem from which she quotes is this:

> I prithee spare me, gentle boy,
> Press me no more for that slight toy,
> That foolish trifle of an heart;
> I swear it will not do its part,
> Though thou dost thine, employ'st thy power and art.
>
> For through long custom it has known
> The little secrets, and is grown
> Sullen and wise, will have its will,
> And, like old hawks, pursues that still
> That makes least sport, flies only where't can kill.
>
> Some youth that has not made his story,
> Will think, perchance, the pain's the glory,
> And mannerly sit out love's feast:
> I shall be carving of the best,
> Rudely call for the last course 'fore the rest.
>
> And, oh, when once that course is past,
> How short a time the feast doth last!
> Men rise away, and scarce say grace,

Or civilly once thank the face
That did invite, but seek another place.

It is the song of a jaded rake who neither loves, nor wishes to enjoy the pleasures of courtship, but will rudely take the woman, and move on to another. There are filthier songs attributed to Suckling – 'A Candle' for instance – but the theme is characteristic of the poet. Men's purposes are animal. Once satisfied they are ever inconsistent. Pleasure in love is ever transitory: 'How short a time the feast doth last.' If Millamant's mind is running on marriage with Mirabell, she might find the theme confirmed in his transitory passion for Mrs Fainall. If she thinks on the wedded state in general, she might consider Mr Fainall as an example of a husband. Nothing can be worse than to be tied for life to a partner of whom one is weary to death. Sir John Suckling is merely voicing one aspect of that deep cynicism concerning sexual relations which underlies the hostility of Restoration comedy to so much of the institution of marriage. One representative quotation must serve to widen the context of the poem: Rhodophil on his wife from the first act of *Marriage à la Mode* in a passage proleptic of Congreve's proviso scene:

> All that I know of her perfections now, is only by memory; I remember, indeed, that about two years ago I loved her passionately; but those golden days are gone . . . . Yet I loved her a whole half year, double the natural term of any mistress, and think in my conscience I could have held out another quarter; but then the world began to laugh at me, and a certain shame of being out of fashion seized me. At last, we arrived at that point that there was nothing left in us to make us new to one another. Yet still I set a good face upon the matter, and am infinite fond of her before company; but, when we are alone, we walk like lions in a room, she one way and I another, and we lie with our backs to each other so far distant as if the fashion of great beds was only invented to keep husband and wife sufficiently asunder.

How is such an 'unfortunate circumstance' to be avoided? Millamant's only power to control her lover is her cruelty; and once marry and that power will evaporate. Moreover, what the worldly-wise Halifax called the 'inequality' of the sexes in marriage was commonly understood to imply that the jaded husband might seek relief elsewhere – an 'habitual' 'fraility' *Advice to a Daughter* calls it — whereas the woman might not so readily hazard her reputation. Make the best of a bad job was the essence of Halifax's view of a married woman's lot, but Millamant enters the proviso scene determined to negotiate for herself better terms than the world might expect, and either keep the love of her husband, or at least retain her integrity and liberty.

After Sir Wilfull, Mirabell appears indeed like 'Phoebus'. It is the right moment to press his claims with grace and wit. The ability of the lovers reciprocally to catch each other's thought and mood is shown with economy by Congreve when Mirabell caps Millamant's verse on his entry. Once again the poem which is being utilized is worth quoting in its entirety. We have moved from Suckling to Edmund Waller's (1606 – 87) *The Story of Phoebus and Daphne Applied*:

> Thyrsis, a youth of the inspirèd train,
> Fair Saccharissa loved, but loved in vain;
> Like Phoebus sung the no less am'rous boy;
> Like Daphne she, as lovely and as coy!
> With numbers he the flying nymph pursues,
> With numbers such as Phoebus' self might use!
> Such is the chase when Love and Fancy leads,
> O'er craggy mountains, and through flow'ry meads;
> Invoked to testify the lover's care,
> Or form some image of his cruel fair.
> Urged with his fury, like a wounded deer,
> O'er these he fled; and now approaching near,
> Had reach'd the nymph with his harmonious lay,
> Whom all his charms could not incline to stay.
> Yet what he sung in his immortal strain,
> Though unsuccessful, was not sung in vain;
> All, but the nymph that should redress his wrong,
> Attend his passion, and approve his song.
> Like Phoebus thus, acquiring unsought praise,
> He catch'd at love, and fill'd his arms with bays.

The original classical myth concerned an attempted rape. Daphne only maintained her chastity by being changed into a laurel. The tale as re-applied by Waller has become a praise of the art occasioned by perpetual courtship. The mistress maintains her 'cruelty' by always fleeing. The chase is both of love and perpetual fancy.

The appropriateness of the lines to Millamant's condition is obvious. But to deny her love for ever is described by Waller as 'wrong'. It is also – in Mirabell's view – contrary to 'instinct'. He thus turns the myth yet another way:

> Do you lock yourself up from me, to make my search more curious?
> Or is this pretty artifice continued, to signify that here the chase must
> end and my pursuit be crowned, for you can fly no further?

But Millamant's choice of the poem is essentially because it is about love as a perpetual chase: she desires to be solicited after marriage as well as before, both for the positive delight which this will bring, and to avoid that sterility breeding contempt which is the condition of so many marriages: 'that love should ever die before us; and that the man so often should out-live the lover' (II. 9 – 11).

These attitudes are the immediate context of the proviso scene, and the reasons behind Millamant's paradoxical insistence on distance and formality in her marriage: 'let us be as strange as if we had been married a great while, and as well-bred as if we were not married at all.' Only by maintaining a certain distance, and by insisting on her own will, pleasure, and above all 'liberty' can she be sure to sustain her role as Daphne to Mirabell's Phoebus. Mirabell's provisos, on the other hand, are intended to establish proper bounds to that freedom, so that strangeness does not degenerate to indifference, and liberty to licence. Although the debate brims over with playful wit, it is the logical outcome of all that has been said earlier in the play about the relation of the sexes and their struggle for power. The intelligence and resilience of the lovers enables Congreve to achieve the prospect of a happy union without denying the force of the cynicism of the Restoration 'comic' view of the satiety and dishonesty of marriage.

Whether this kind of balanced relationship was Congreve's 'ideal' view of sex can never be known. Since he himself never married, preferring the delights of another man's wife, he may have been, like Mr Fainall, a refiner on his pleasures. In any case, the proviso scene is highly conventional. It derives, among other sources, from Honoré D'Urfé's handbook for gallantry L'Astrée (1607 – 27). The contract between Hylas and Stelle there (drawn up before witnesses) likewise banished all expressions of endearment and insisted on liberty of speech and action.

An agreed absence of jealousy was a necessary concomitant, however, to a mutual right of inconstancy. Dryden incorporated proviso material in *The Wild Gallant* (1663), *Secret Love* (1667), *Marriage à la Mode* (1672) and *Amphitryon* (1690). The device had been used for broader comic effect in James Howard's *All Mistaken* (1667) and Edward Ravenscroft's *The Careless Lovers* (1673) and *The Canterbury Guests* (1694). It is a commonplace of such scenes that the relation of mistress and gallant was a securer basis for happiness than the dull assurance of husband and wife. So important is the tradition, and Congreve's development of it, that a major representative analogue is worth quotation:

Florimell   But this marriage is such a bugbear to me; much might be if we could invent but any way to make it easy.

Celadon   Some foolish people have made it uneasy, by drawing the knot faster than they need; but we that are wiser will loosen it a little . . . As for the first year according to the laudable custom of new married people, we shall follow one another up into chambers and down into gardens, and think we shall never have enough of one another. So far 'tis pleasant enough I hope.

Florimell   But after that, when we begin to live like husband and wife, and never come near one another – what then, sir?

Celadon   Why, then our only happiness must be to have one mind, and one will, Florimell.

Florimell   One mind if thou wilt, but prithee let us have two wills; for I find one will be little enough for me alone; but how if those wills should meet and clash, Celadon?

Celadon   I warrant thee for that. Husbands and wives keep their wills far enough asunder for ever meeting. One thing let us be sure to agree on, that is, never to be jealous.

Florimell   No, but e'en love one another as long as we can; and confess the truth when we can love no longer.

Celadon   When I have been at play, you shall never ask me what money I have lost.

Florimell   When I have been abroad you shall never enquire who treated me.

Celadon   *Item*, I will have liberty to sleep all night, without your interrupting my repose for any evil design whatsoever.

Florimell   *Item*, then you shall bid me goodnight before you sleep.

Celadon Provided always, that whatever liberties we take with other people, we continue very honest to one another.
Florimell As far as will consist with a pleasant life.
Celadon Lastly, whereas the names of husband and wife hold forth nothing, but clashing and cloying, and dulness and faintness in their signification, they shall be abolished for ever betwixt us.
Florimell And instead of those, we will be married by the more agreeable names of Mistress and Gallant.   (*Secret Love* V.i. 530 – 76)

Dryden's and Congreve's provisos are closest in their insistence on liberty. Florimell's and Celadon's definition of marriage, the characters agree, is as good as wenching, but it has the disadvantage of that pastime also: Celadon considers it may be his fortune to be made a cuckold, and his proclivity for gaming is accepted as a *quid pro quo*. In comparison, Mirabell wishes to prevent liberty degenerating into licentiousness with his own provisos that 'I may not be beyond measure enlarged into a husband' (i.e. cuckold), and his insistence that Millamant's 'acquaintance' shall be 'general' only. Millamant's 'Detestable *imprimis*! I go to the play in a mask!' must be seen in this context. Her first explanation misleads (as she often intends) by seeming to object to her husband's restrictions. The second qualifies this by revealing what she finds truly detestable: the suggestion that she might be the kind of woman who went in disguise to a rendezvous with a lover. It is a pledge of her chastity, therefore, but expressed by implication which makes Florimell's mind pedestrian in comparison. The same twist is exercised with Millamant's word 'liberty': 'My dear liberty, shall I leave thee?' Which is probably intended to suggest a similar sexual innuendo to that in Dryden, and then turned comically and harmlessly with: 'I can't do it, 'tis more than impossible. Positively, Mirabell I'll lie abed in a morning as long as I please.'

If some of Millamant's provisos are – at least, in their fancifulness – more extreme than Florimell's and Celadon's: she will not even have a year of the laudable custom of being together with her husband, on the other hand the resolution of the opposition of the lovers' two wills in Congreve is far more recognizable as a normative happy marriage. Witness Mirabell's reference to children, totally excluded by Dryden. The act of sex itself is turned to comedy by both writers, but the 'odious endeavours' in Congreve are directed to procreation whereas Celadon seems as much repulsed as attracted by the 'liberty' of the act. The man says he does not want to be wakened in the night to service the woman's desires, and she agrees not to trouble him provided she can be fucked each night before he falls asleep. It is a clockwork view of the processes of desire.

The greater length of the proviso scene in Congreve enables him to enter in more detail into the minutia of married existence – the regime of the tea-table, make-up, drink, the problem of relatives whom one dislikes, the needs for privacy. There is an element in the episode which suggests a manual for married etiquette. Unlike the uneasy gallantry of Dryden's rakish couple, the talk of Congreve's lovers is full of what Johnson found in Shakespeare: 'practical axioms and domestic wisdom'. As important as the content is the manner. The solemn, inflexible face which Mirabell wore when he failed to win Millamant has gone. Instead we find graceful badinage, paradox and fantasy. The manner may remind us that Congreve and Joseph Addison were friends, and the reformative comedy of the *Spectator* papers is suggested by this scene. It would be mistaken to credit the new morality of Congreve's lovers to the moral blasts of Jeremy Collier's *Immorality and Profaneness of the English Stage* (1698). Social and literary attitudes had certainly been changing since the accession of William and Mary,[15] and Mirabell is reformed compared with a Restoration rake like Dorimant, or even the young men of *The Old Bachelor*, but the tone is still very much of a hard-headed wit. Collier's cantankerous, Bible-ridden, puritanical hostility to the stage is quite irrelevant to these young lovers.

The worldly-wise will appreciate the irony of Mrs Fainall's entry to close the episode, and Millamant's enquiry to her 'Shall I have him? I think I must have him.' The woman of whom she asks the question has been in the very best position to know what sort of man she recommends: 'Aye, aye, take him, take him, what should you do?' Should there be any intercourse by glances at this juncture between the husband-to-be and his cast mistress? It is a nice directorial point. Such is the deliberate ambiguity of Congreve's writing that we never know if Millamant knows of this relationship. Marwood said that she 'thought there was something in it' and Millamant has probably deduced the breakdown of the Fainalls' marriage. Has she put two and two together? If she has, there is an additional dark irony in her moment of truth with Mrs Fainall:

> Well, if Mirabell should not make a good husband,
> I am a lost thing – for I find I love him violently.

It is one of the rare moments in the play when she drops her masquerade, and speaks sincerely. She cannot be certain of the reciprocity and continuance of Mirabell's love. Can it be that marriage to her, and her fortune, are merely means by which her husband can continue to readily enjoy the company of the woman to whom she speaks these lines? Mrs Fainall's rejoinder is far from sentimental or romantic: 'If you doubt him, you had best take up with Sir Wilfull.' The only way she can be secure of not being deceived is to avoid the most attractive man in her society, and marry a sot. Given these undertones, her affectation even now in refusing to kiss Mirabell on the lips is more than coquetry, or an expression of her desire to be always pursued. It is a sign also of her fear. She is still vulnerable.

5. 'Female frailty': the role and function of Lady Wishfort

Millamant has almost no part to play in the resolution of the comic action. After her engagement she is driven from the scene by the boorish attentions of Petulant and Sir Wilfull and the struggle of the rest of the play centres on money: hers, her aunt's, Mrs Fainall's. The battle between Mirabell and Mr Fainall issues in open hostility. At the centre of the conflict is not the heroine, but her aunt, Lady Wishfort.

The character is both one of the richest and the most difficult roles Congreve created. The type was well established in the comic repertory. Her name recalls Loveit in *The Man of Mode* or Lady Loveyouth in Shadwell's *The Humourists* (1670). Her amorous affectations find parallel in Etherege's Lady Cockwood (*She Would If She Could*, 1668) and Beliza's relations with Bernado in Shadwell's *The Amorous Bigot* (1690), her education of her daughter may be likened to Lady Fantast's conceptions in the same author's *Bury Fair* (1689).

Her signification in *The Way of the World* has been discussed before we first see her. Mirabell is mocking:

> I think the good lady would marry anything that resembled a man, though 'twere no more than what a butler could pinch out of a napkin. (II. 280 – 2)

But Mrs Fainall enlarges the characterization to include her whole sex, and in so doing the context alters from the comic to something recognizable as yet another 'unhappy circumstance' of life:

> Female frailty! We must all come to it, if we live to be old and feel the craving of a false appetite when the true is decayed. (II. 283 – 5)

These lines relate thematically to Millamant's statement that cruelty is power and when a woman parts with these, then she is 'old and ugly'. It is ridiculous to wish to be considered sexually desirable when the passing of time has made one the 'antidote to desire', but it is a circumstance which threatens us all, let us paint the paint an inch thick. Our laughter may not be entirely free of pain, and the humiliation of Lady Wishfort and the 'tyranny' with which she is threatened by Mr Fainall suggest dark possibilities in the action of the play at the end as threatening as the quarrel between Marwood and her lover early in the action. It is problematical whether Congreve successfully holds together at the climax the lighter and darker aspects of the action involving Lady Wishfort.

The verbal exuberance of the character, the extravagance of her behaviour, and the harsh manner in which she is disabused all recall Jonson. Congreve admired the portrayal of Morose in *Epicoene*. That character was gulled into a marriage by his nephew Dauphine with a boy disguised as a girl, and then has to compound for his release with his fortune after repeated humiliation, riot in his house, tales that his wife is a whore, and a forced public protestation of impotence. The viciousness of Dauphine resembles that of Mr Fainall. Having got his way with his uncle, Jonson's character says: 'I'll not trouble you, till you trouble me with your funeral, which I care not how soon it come.'[16] Mirabell's plots, by comparison, are gentle. He deceives with gallantry, and commands with gentleness. But the toughness of the general situation resembles Jonson's manner of purging a 'humour' character.

The different generic decorum in *The Way of the World* makes it impossible, however, for Congreve merely to portray the character as one of the grotesque types of the Jonsonian theatre of comic cruelty. The naturalism, or, perhaps one should use the French term of the day, the *vraisemblance*, of much of the action of Congreve's world, and the nicety of many of his social and moral distinctions, make it difficult to hold a substantially developed character at sufficient distance from life to act merely as a monstrous Aunt Sally. Accordingly, even the most obviously Jonsonian devices change their signification. Consider the tirade with which Foible is dismissed:

> Away! out! out! Go set up for yourself again! Do, drive a trade, do, with your three-pennyworth of small ware, flaunting upon a pack-thread, under a brandy-seller's bulk, or against a dead wall by a ballad-monger! Go, hang out an old frisoneer gorget, with a yard of yellow colberteen again. Do! an old gnawed mask, two rows of pins, and a child's fiddle; a glass necklace with the beads broken, and a quilted nightcap with one ear. Go, go, drive a trade! . . . (V. 9–16)

This invites comparison with the streams of abuse Subtle pours upon Face in *The Alchemist*: the graphic social detail, the force and animus of the comic outrage, the verbal inventiveness, even the very length of the catalogue, all are recognizably Jonsonian. But this kind of speech is not common with other characters in *The Way of the World*. The only major exception is Marwood's account of the ills of scandal to Lady Wishfort (V. 193–206), but this catalogue is created to fit Lady Wishfort's ambience. It is possible, therefore, that Congreve had created for the old lady a style of speech which is far more special for her in this play than it would be in Jonson where rhetorical excess is widespread. Thus the energy, inventiveness, the ability to dramatize a situation with verbal fantasy seem to spring from *within* this character, and are hence even qualities which one may admire in her especially since they resemble, *mutatis mutandis*, certain qualities of mind and speech which we detect in her niece Millamant.

Since Congreve had knit a web of family relationship which is extremely close in this play – the majority of the principals are related by birth or marriage – the possibility must be considered that a similarity between aunt and niece is thematically functional. Both practise extremes of affectation and coquetry. Millamant's declaration that she pins up her hair with lovers' verses goes beyond the excesses of powder and paint in the older lady. Lady Wishfort supine on a sofa with one foot jogging off the end is no more ridiculous than Millamant refusing to kiss the man she has just agreed to marry. Both are equally attracted by Mirabell, and both deceived by him, the aunt by his pretended addresses, the niece by his affair with Mrs Fainall. The difference of our reaction is strongly conditioned merely by the difference in age and sexual attraction, but such 'female frailty' if continued when the grace of youth is past and one is 'old and ugly' might well turn Millamant into the type which her aunt represents.

Another parallel may be observed between Lady Wishfort and her daughter (Mrs Fainall). Their hunger for men leads to a breach of decorum. Mrs Fainall laments rather than mocks with Mirabell the green sickness of women, because the ridicule lights close to herself. Congreve goes out of his way to inform us that she had been a widow less than a year before she married again, and since she feared she was with child by Mirabell at this time, her sexual hunger is as rampant as that of a Gertrude for a Claudius. Her mother's eagerness to bed with Sir Rowland is of the same nature. Again, both women are deceived by Mirabell. It is in his power to seduce the whole family. He cheats the mother, has an affair with the daughter, and marries the niece.

Is this a general satiric comment by Congreve on the nature of women, or merely the result of his defective imagination — he could only conceive women of a certain type? For instance, the lustful widow is a traditional figure, and Congreve may have been working merely variations on an old theme with Lady Wishfort and Mrs Fainall because he was unable to produce anything else. Doubtless there will be those who see the play as giving a limited man's eye view of the faults of the opposite sex. Be that as it may, these limitations, whether in the writer or in the women, are of major importance in the play. Since the subject is the seduction or the courtship of women, the passionate principle of sexuality is central to the action.

It follows that one must enquire whether, ultimately, the central character of the piece is Lady Wishfort? The excess of her sexual desire which precipitates all sorts of folly, and her eventual humiliation, strongly suggest that her role in the play is closely akin to the kind of dominant comic protagonist one finds in Jonson (or Molière). She conditions the action throughout, even from the first scene where we learn that it is her control over Millamant which is an essential determinant of the action. Her first appearance directly follows an episode with Millamant and acts as a neo-Falstaffian comment on coquetry. Thereafter, more and more, she comes to dominate the action; especially it is her presence, her utterances and reactions, which control the tone of the final act even though it is Mirabell and Mr Fainall who manipulate the plot.

Given this importance, it is not surprising that Congreve gives her a remarkable range. The Jonsonian force of her utterance has already been noted, but would one necessarily conclude that the following passages were also spoken by the same character?

> Well, Sir Rowland, you have the way. You are no novice in the labyrinth of love; you have the clue. But as I am a person, Sir Rowland, you must not attribute my yielding to any sinister appetite or indigestion of widowhood; nor impute my complacency to any lethargy of continence. I hope you do not think me prone to any iteration of nuptials.
> (IV. 469–74)

. . . .

Well, nephew, upon your account – ah, he has a false insinuating tongue! Well, sir, I will stifle my just resentment at my nephew's request. I will endeavour what I can to forget, but on proviso that you resign the contract with my niece immediately . . .

(*aside*) Oh, he has witchcraft in his eyes and tongue! When I did not see him, I could have bribed a villain to his assassination; but his appearance rakes the embers which have so long lain smothered in my breast.   (V. 370 *f*)

The second passage relates to Mirabell. It is stripped of the verbal energy and fantasy of the tirade at Foible (or at Mirabell: III 114–21). The reference to 'just resentment' is fair and apposite. The lady has been notoriously abused, and the commitment of Waitwell to prison, and the threat of Bridewell for Foible, have been proper reminders that society recognizes rights and laws which Mirabell has overstepped. Lady Wishfort stands upon those rights and her place in the family hierarchy. She acts too with a directness and simplicity which spring from her recognition of her place, and which shows the practicality of a woman who could at least handle Sir Wilfull sober or drunk. At the same time love betrays her. She recognizes *veteris vestigia flammae* – the traces of the old passion – and the language in which she expresses this, though mannered, strikes one as sincere. It may be folly for age to love youth, but the sentiment rings true, and she is not here ridiculed in a Jonsonian manner. On the contrary, if we do not feel for her, we may at least understand the nature of her predicament. It is just as real for her and dangerous as Millamant's.

How differently this has developed from the way the speech to Sir Rowland would have led one to predict. That showed *préciosité* gone beserk, a conglomeration of periphrases for sexual frustration and desire which are utterly ridiculous and which exactly fit Mirabell's characterization of her as willing to marry even a napkin in the shape of a man. In her Jonsonian tirades Lady Wishfort was in control of the comic language, but here she has lost both mastery of words and sense in a euphemistic pedantry of lust. Before her looking-glass, in an earthy and inventive mood, with devastating self-knowledge and self-directed ridicule, she could mock herself as 'arrantly flayed . . . like an old peeled wall'. Wish-fulfilment now intoxicates as she babbles of 'iteration of nuptials'.

This kind of verbal range is not found in any other character in the play. Possibly Congreve merely uses her in different places to respond in whatever way the changing comic situation demands, but the very continuance of one actress's presence in different scenes with a role as developed as this, will imply a central core of personality which resists reduction of role merely to function, and the intuitions which *vraisemblance* provoke will be called upon to seek unity behind diversity, and hence discover complexity in the character. Lady Wishfort is a creation of the 'humour' tradition of artificial comedy who acts at times sincerely in a naturalistic mode, and is called upon at the climax of the action to respond to a situation which veers from comedy to melodrama and even, potentially, towards tragedy. (One might compare Alcéste in Molière). Let us consider the resolution of the play.

6. The denouement: Act V

Perhaps the strain generated in the comic structure in the last act is too great. There is an animus and a reality about the evil of Marwood and Mr Fainall which works against generic decorum. When Mr Fainall draws his sword on his wife, his desire to kill her appears the genuine product of the frustrations, tensions and hate which have been building up throughout the play, and the *deus ex machina* of the black box, if it solves Mirabell's difficulties, is not credible as a means of reconciling the Fainalls to their marriage. The nastiness of the threatened scandal, even the introduction of matters of law, contribute towards a naturalistic sense of bitterness. In this situation Congreve continually uses Lady Wishfort to re-establish comic norms against the tragic potentialities, though even she (as we have seen) at moments speaks with a moving sincerity.

The resolution of these tragi-comic tensions issues in melodrama. The mixture of modes recalls *The Double Dealer*. In that play Congreve had relied on an element of deliberate staginess to obviate difficulties. The audience were reminded that they were watching a play, and thus, since this is an entertainment of artifice, they would more readily adjust to the shifts of decorum than if the illusion of *vraisemblance* were maintained throughout. In *The Way of the World* Marwood's soliloquy (III. 201 *f*) is important in the same way. It was a favoured (and unnaturalistic) device with Maskwell in the earlier play. Here the very artificiality of Marwood suddenly addressing the audience effects an abrupt change of mode:

> Indeed, Mrs Engine, is it thus with you? Are you become a go-between of this importance? Yes, I shall watch you. . . . The devil's an ass; if I were a painter, I would draw him like an idiot, a driveler with a bib and bells. Man should have his head and horns, and woman the rest of him. Poor simple fiend!

She declares herself a satiric philosopher, and speaks like a villainess. Her name and function are allegorically united, and in the artifice of soliloquy she is stripped of her naturalistic qualities and is reduced to a personification. Further emphasis on the staginess of this is provided by direct allusion to the title of Jonson's play *The Devil is an Ass* (1616), the intrigue of which directly parallels that of the Fainalls. It is important that Congreve having stereotyped her in this manner should continue to use her thereafter in this way. Probably to confirm her merely as a negative force – she who would mar all (herself included) – the scene with Millamant follows. This culminates in the bitchiness of the younger lover's song: 'If there's delight in love, 'tis when I see / The heart, which others bleed for, bleed for me.' This shows Millamant's 'cruelty', but its prime function is to apply that cruelty to a proper object, the villainess. The cutting up of Marwood here does not move sympathy. The purpose is to confirm her in her fixed sexual hatred of the 'heroine' and to drive her to actions which are beyond the pale.

When Mr Fainall kisses Marwood in reconciliation (III.631) we should, hence, not interpret the action naturalistically as an expression of love, but rather as an indication that he is making a pact with evil for a destructive purpose. He himself is also reduced to a type: the jealous cuckold.

> Why then, Foible's a bawd, an arrant, rank, match-making bawd.
> And I, it seems, am a husband, a rank husband; and my wife a very
> arrant, rank wife, all in the way of the world.   (III. 552 – 55)

This obliterates nicety of discrimination in a triad of pander, whore, and cuckold, and, as with Marwood, the excess of sexual hate this provokes resolves Mr Fainall to break the decorum of deceptive propriety and engineer a scandal for mercenary ends. Both the characters, therefore, at the culmination of the play are less than fully human, mechanized in some degree by their anger, and bent on social disruption. According to the conventions of comic theatre they are being set up to be defeated.

The staginess of the ending is further emphasized by Congreve's use of Witwoud's lines: 'Heyday! what, are you all got together, like players at the end of the last act?' The tricks and counter-tricks of the plot at this point have been occurring with such improbable rapidity, it is no great jolt to the theatrical illusion to be reminded that this is all play-acting and that the laws of naturalistic probability were suspended some time ago. By Witwoud's entry we are already listening for the music of the dance which will (hopefully) end all in an image of social reconciliation and harmony. The lines run the risk even of being inopportune in their obviousness. That is why they are given to Witwoud, for they turn out to be yet another of his comic similitudes.

Yet it is not easy successfully to effect the transition of mode and mood by which, as it were, people in whose affairs we have grown concerned are turned into types in a theatrical structure. This play had demanded frequently that we give the same alert, intuitive attention to speech and emotion as we give to real life. Convincing emotions, important moral or social attitudes have continually given generic convention the semblance of truth. The very actors and actresses are people not puppets and must inevitably bring to complex roles a sense of real personality experienced in life. It is very difficult for a dramatist to change direction by twisting what seems human into the terms of artistic convention. Consider Mr Fainall's lines:

> This, my Lady Wishfort, must be subscribed, or your darling daughter's turned adrift, like a leaky hulk, to sink or swim, as she and the current of this lewd town can agree.

or the mother's:

> Why, have you not been naught? Have you not been sophisticated? Not understand? Here am I ruined to compound for your caprices and your cuckoldoms. I must pawn my plate and jewels, and ruin my niece, and all little enough.

Certain phrases here insist on committing feeling and truth to them: 'darling daughter', 'this lewd town', 'Not understand?' 'all little enough' – these demand an emotional engagement with something that sounds real and serious.

Hence the crucial importance of Lady Wishfort's role in the play's structure. The final act has to be built round the central comic character. She has been so strongly established both as the butt of our mirth and the creator of a richly specific and spawningly humorous vocabulary, that the expectation is that whatever happens, *this* character cannot be the participant in a tragic resolution. Her function, thus, is very similar, to that of Dogberry *vis à vis* Don John in *Much Ado About Nothing*, though Congreve has moved Lady Wishfort from the periphery to the centre of his action. Consider, for instance, a speech directly conducive of laughter, such as the following to Marwood:

> O my dear friend, how can I enumerate the benefits that I have

received from your goodness? To you I owe the timely discovery of
the false vows of Mirabell; to you the detection of the imposter Sir
Rowland. And now you are become an intercessor with my son-in-
law, to save the honour of my house, and compound for the frailties of
my daughter. Well, friend, you are enough to reconcile me to the bad
world, or else I would retire to deserts and solitudes, and feed
harmless sheep by groves and purling streams. Dear Marwood, let us
leave the world, and retire by ourselves and be shepherdesses.

The first part of this speech is susceptible to analysis in terms of some of
the earlier naturalistic scenes of the play. 'Friend' is, as usual, a danger
signal. (Consider the cut and thrust round the word between Marwood
and Mrs Fainall which immediately follows). One might claim that Lady
Wishfort betrays a lack of prudent suspicion of the ways of the world by
not asking what Marwood's motive might be in continually revealing
these plots to her, or interceding for the honour of her house. But such
reflections are diverted by the latter part of the speech which merely
romps into a rhapsody which might be categorized as a deliberate fantasy
from Millamant, but which in her aunt suggests rather a woolly-minded
collapse into a romantic mode: 'Dear Marwood, let us leave the world,
and retire by ourselves and be shepherdesses.' This is (unintentional)
pastoral burlesque. Possibly one might moralize about the utterance by
observing that there is no escape from this world (except to the
Wrekin!), and that Lady Wishfort ought, instead, to learn to manipulate
life as it is. But her expression, primarily, will simply produce laughter.

The villains, therefore, have to work *against* a series of laughs produced
by the old lady: witness, especially, the long sequence on Mrs Fainall's
education which turns mother and daughter into extravagant caricatures.
On the other hand, Mirabell's plots work *for* a comic, rather than tragic,
conclusion, and thus he functions generically in phase with Lady
Wishfort. One finds a continual tension between lines like Lady Wishfort's plea that she might be married 'but in case of necessity, as of health,
or some such emergency' and Mrs Fainall's sneers and tyrannical
demands which are far from comic. Whereas Mirabell's playful *précieux*
flattery – 'Nay, kill me not, by turning from me in disdain' – moves
the old lady back into her comic role of the aged coquette, which is pleas-
ing to her, and delightful to the audience.

The transitions of mode, the mixture of laughter and viciousness, caricature and character, are so frequent that verbal analysis would become offensively tedious if it limped through them all. The effectiveness, in any case, can only be tested by practical experiment. The complexity of the task Congreve has set himself is rich with opportunities. It is problematical whether he always succeeds.

The mixture of mode is maintained until the end. The dance in comedy is traditionally the emblem of hymen and communicates to the ear as well as eye the idea of harmony. Concerning Millamant and Mirabell this generic expectation is fulfilled. The sequential dialogue, which serves by way of dramatic epilogue, does not convince, however, that hymeneal or harmonious principles will extend through the rest of 'the world'.

> *Lady Wishfort* As I am a person, I can hold out no longer. I have wasted my spirits so today already that I am ready to sink under the fatigue; and I cannot but have some fears upon me yet that my son Fainall will pursue some desperate course.
> *Mirabell* Madam, disquiet not yourself on that account; to my knowledge his circumstances are such, he must of force comply. For my part, I will contribute all that in me lies to a reunion. In the meantime, madam (*To* Mrs Fainall.), let me before these witnesses restore to you this deed of trust; it may be a means, well-managed, to make you live easily together.
>
> From hence let those be warned, who mean to wed,
> Lest mutual falsehood stain the bridal bed;
> For each deceiver to his cost may find,
> That marriage frauds too oft are paid in kind.

Age, in the person of Lady Wishfort, drops out of the hymeneal dance first, thus ending it. The words 'I can hold out no longer' may be understood allegorically since the dance suggests something of the generic formality of masque. She confesses that she can no longer play the role of beloved mistress, and will be reconciled to widowhood and celibacy. As she is a 'person' however − rather than an allegorical representation of age − do we really credit that her dance of folly is over? Only moments before she has addressed Mrs Fainall thus: 'O daughter, daughter, 'tis plain thou hast inherited thy mother's prudence.' Such words are not indicative of the maturity of disenchanted self-knowledge. We may guess, therefore, that she remains what she always was, and the comedy does not put an end formally to folly by the easy device of showing it disabused, and verbally declaring it to have ceased.

On the contrary, Congreve stimulates the imagination to consider the world of the subsequent action. Will Mr Fainall, for example, 'pursue some desperate course'? Mirabell would seem the last person likely to persuade him to a reunion. As for Mrs Marwood – nobody dare say anything. Her last words had been a vow of revenge, and if her will is greater than her ability to conceive the means, we may presume, nonetheless, that she is not deprived of her malicious tongue: 'If it must all come out . . . 'tis but the way of the world' her lover had admitted.

The one instrument of power to restrain the villainous couple is the deed of trust which now gives Mrs Fainall financial control over her husband. For a wife to be able to destroy her husband in this way may be a check on separation, but one may be sceptical how far this may make them 'live easily together'. In Mirabell's cynical view 'tis the way of the world . . . of the widows of the world' and one should note that he echoes Mr Fainall's earlier words. Thus even at the end, as at the beginning, there is a similarity between the two men. No one would suggest that either of them has a romantic view of love. One of the means by which Mirabell wins this final game with Mr Fainall is that he is the cooler, perhaps one should say the colder, man. His mistress gives him thanks as 'a cautious friend'. The noun, as always, is ambiguous; the adjective exact.

One nice point about the Fainalls is that Mirabell's ex-mistress is saved from a public scandal, whatever Marwood may risk whispering behind her back. Since Millamant is on stage during the row it is just as well that Mrs Fainall can state to Marwood:'You have aspersed me wrongfully. I have proved your falsehood.' This is a direct lie, of course, but it saves face. Thus Millamant can enter marriage believing, publicly at least, that Mr Fainall and Marwood invented the story of her husband's affair with Mrs Fainall, while, on the contrary, the villains' liaison is proved and confessed. Moreover, Mrs Fainall has another hold over her husband and his mistress if frenzy provokes Marwood to scandal. It is a nasty weapon, and in dishonest hands, but such is the way of the world.

Mirabell's concluding pair of couplets apply, therefore, directly to the Fainalls. They are of general application also. Their formality suggests that the lines will be delivered directly to the audience as convention requires. The barrier between spectator and spectacle is broken down, and the moral of the play is applied to the theatre of the world.

Congreve scoffed at Collier's 'political arithmetic' which saw the action on the stage as a microcosm of all society.[17] It was a fair debating point. It is a very small section of society with which the comedy is concerned, and in a very limited relationship. The 'world' is confined to a handful of smart families in the wealthier parts of London, and their activities in sex and love. It would be naive to see this as encompassing all Restoration high society, or to confuse the conventions of art with real life. Yet Congreve's aim is specifically declared to be general satire – witness the formal declaration of the play's epilogue – and Richard Steele likewise observed in his commendatory verses to the play:

> The player acts the world, the world the player.

Deceit and mutual rancour in marriage, sexual promiscuity without lasting love; the pursuit of power by physical charm or financial control; endless duplicity and hypocrisy; affectation, vanity: these are the ways of the world, gilded often with the graces of wit and good manners. The society portrayed has the morality of the jungle and the artificiality of a court. 'The language is everywhere that of Men of Honour, but their Actions are those of Knaves' was the judgement not of Collier, but of Voltaire.[18]

Since this is comic theatre, we must presume that Millamant and Mirabell will secure happiness in their treaty of marriage through mutual fidelity and respect enhanced by beauty, charm, intelligence and wit. They are skilled and hard enough to survive the ways of the world. But, as Congreve observed, the characters of comedy are imperfect (as in real life), and even though Millamant and Mirabell are the hymeneal couple whom the final dance celebrates, one should weigh the man's last words to the woman:

> I would have you as often as possibly I can. (*Kisses her hand.*)
> Well, heaven grant I love you not too well; that's all my fear.

That last sentence parallels Millamant's 'Well, if Mirabell should not make a good husband, I am a lost thing – for I find I love him violently.' As a husband Mirabell has good reason not to love too well a woman whose craving for liberty matches his own, and whose whirlwind of affected coquetry, though it charms, may degenerate too easily if indulged too far. That is why he fears to love too well. Even in his highest compliment, he shows a disenchanted view of romance.

Notes

[1] All quotations are from Kathleen M. Lynch's edition (Regents Restoration Drama Series, 1965) to which I am generally indebted for scholarly information.

[2] For the libertine ethos of Restoration comedy generally see D. Underwood, *Etherege and the Seventeenth-Century Comedy of Manners* (Yale Studies in English 135, 1957).

[3] In 'Amendments of Mr Collier's False and Imperfect Citations . . .' (1698), text from B. Dobrées World's Classics edn of *The Mourning Bride*, etc., p. 453.

[4] *Op.cit.*, n.3, p. 408: '*Comedy* (says *Aristotle*) is an Imitation of the worse sort of People. Μιμησις φαυλοτξρων, imitatio pejorum. He does not mean the worse sort of People in respect to their Quality, but in respect to their Manners. . . . the Vices most frequent, and which are the Common Practice of the looser sort of Livers, are the Subject Matter of Comedy.'

[5] *La Practique du Théâtre* (Amsterdam, 1715), p. 64. Congreve possessed two copies of Hédélin's treatise, one in French, the other in English. See J. Hodges's catalogue, *The Library of William Congreve* (1955).

[6] See further D.S. Berkeley '*Préciosité* and the Restoration Comedy of Manners', *Huntington Library Quarterly 18* (1954 – 5), C.D. Cecil, 'Libertine and *Précieux* Elements in Restoration Comedy '*Essays in Criticism 9* (1950).

[7] *Of Dramatic Poetry and Other Critical Essays* ed. G. Watson (1962), I, 72.

[8] *Epicoene*, Everyman edn of Jonson's plays, I, 526.

[9] Regents Restoration Drama Series, ed. W.B. Carnochan (1966).

[10] The speaker is a shoe-maker, but he is likening himself to the gentry.

[11] *An Apology for the Life of Mr Colley Cibber*, ed. R.W. Lowe (1889), I, 173.

[12] See J.H. Smith, *The Gay Couple in Restoration Comedy* (1948).

[13] Penguin edn of Halifax's *Works* ed. J.P. Kenyon, p. 278.

[14] So Carolina to Lovel in Shadwell's *The Sullen Lovers* (1668): 'pray you, sir, leave off; I had rather hear a silenced parson preach sedition, than you talk seriously of love. Would you could see how it becomes you; why, you look more comically than an old-fashioned

fellow singing of Robin Hood of Chevy Chase. . . . Come, in what posture must I stand to hear you talk formally?' (II.i). See also Hédélin op.cit. n.3, pp. 262-2 on the inappropriateness of moral maxims in comedy.

15 The issues are extremely complicated. There is an excellent brief summary of the shifting position in M.E. Novak's *William Congreve* (1971), pp. 48*f*. More general accounts of the relations of literature and society in the age are J.W. Krutch, *Comedy and Conscience after the Restoration* (rev. edn. 1949); J. Loftis, *Comedy and Society from Congreve to Fielding* (1959); K.M. Lynch, *The Social Mode of Restoration Comedy* (1926); and feminists will find interesting material in J.E. Gagen, *The New Woman: Her Emergence in English Drama 1660-1730* (1954).

16 *Epicoene*, n.8, p. 557.

17 'Amendments of Mr Collier's . . .', n.3, p. 412. Congreve mocks the line of reasoning which claims 'the Stage is the Image of the World; by the Men and Women represented there, are signified all the Men and Women in the World; so that if four Women are shewn upon the Stage, and three of them are vicious, it is as much as to say, that three parts in four of the whole Sex are stark naught.'

18 *Letters Concerning the English Nation* 19 (1733).

Further Reading

Background
E.L. Avery, *Congreve's Plays on the Eighteenth-Century Stage* (1951)
J.C. Hodges, *William Congreve the Man* (1941)
Critical. My principal debts are to:
I. Donaldson, *The World Upside-Down* (1970)
J.Gagen, 'Congreve's Mirabell and the Ideal of the Gentleman',
   Publications of the Modern Language Association 79 (1964)
H. Hawkins, *Likeness of Truth in Elizabethan and Restoration Drama*
(1972)
C. Leech, 'Congreve and the Century's End' *Philological Quarterly* 41
   (1962)
B. Morris ed., *William Congreve* (Mermaid Critical Commentaries,
1972)
P. and M. Mueschke, *A New View of Congreve's 'Way of the World'* (1958)
K. Muir, 'The Comedies of William Congreve' *Restoration Theatre*
   (Stratford-upon-Avon Studies 6, ed. J.R. Brown and B. Harris, 1965)
M.E. Novak, *William Congreve* (1971)

Index

Addison, Joseph 45
affectation 16, 17, 19, 30, 31, 32, 36, 37, 38, 46, 49, 59
Aristotle 12, 60n.4

Beaumont and Fletcher 32
Betterton, Thomas 9
Bracegirdle, Anne 30
Byron, Lord 36

Chekhov, Anton 26
Churchill, John 34
Cibber, Colley 30, 60n.11
Collier, Jeremy 25, 45, 59, 60n.3, 61n.17
comic convention 7, 16, 26, 27, 33, 42, 54, 58, 59
Congreve, William: *The Old Bachelor* 9, 10, 45;
Letter Concerning Humour in Comedy 30;
Love for Love 9, 12, 13, 16, 34, 38;
The Double Dealer 13, 18, 53
Cowley, Abraham: *The Cutter of Coleman Street* 16

decorum 7, 11, 48, 49, 53, 54
Dryden John, 21, 43, 44, 45;
Marriage à la Mode 38, 40, 43;
The Wild Gallant 43;
Amphitryon 43;
Secret Love 43–4
Dennis, John, 30
D'Urfé, Honoré: *L'Astrée* 42

Elizabethan plays 16

Epicureanism 10, 11
Etherege, Sir George 60n. 2;
The Man of Mode 27, 28, 47;
She Would if She Could 47

Falstaff 50
genre/generic conventions 16, 26, 27, 29, 30, 48, 53, 55, 56–7

Halifax, Lord 40, 41, 60n. 13;
Advice to a Daughter 34, 41
Hédélin, François 12, 60n.5, n.14
Hobbes, Thomas 34
Horace 32, 37, 38
Howard, James: *All Mistaken* 43
'humours' 7, 31, 48, 52

James, Henry 15
Johnson, Dr 45
Jonson, Ben 7, 16, 28, 31, 33, 35, 37, 48, 50, 51;
Volpone (The Fox) 12, 35;
Epicoene 33, 48, 60n.8, 61n.16;
The Alchemist 49;
The Devil is an Ass 54

libertine 9, 11, 17, 18, 25, 26, 60n.2, n.6

Machiavellianism 7, 12, 13, 33, 36
manners 7, 15, 19
Marlowe, Christopher: *The Jew of Malta* 12
masque 57
Molière 36, 50, 52

money 9, 11, 12, 13, 16, 18, 27, 34, 35, 47
More, Sir Thomas 32

naturalism 26, 27, 30, 48, 52, 53, 54, 56

Pope, Alexander 38
préciosité 14, 33, 36, 51, 56, 60n.6
'provisos' 17, 33, 34, 37, 41, 42–3, 44

Ravenscroft,: *The Careless Lovers* 43;
    The Canterbury Ghosts 43
Restoration Comedy 17, 38;
    themes of 9, 10;
    ethical norms of 9, 12, 26, 28;
    comic norms 9, 26, 42, 53;
    sexual morality 20, 27, 40
romantic conventions 24, 27, 30, 34, 58

satirical elements 18, 25, 31, 37, 38, 49, 53, 59
Shadwell, Thomas 60n.14;
    The Humourists 47;
    The Amorous Bigot 47;
    Bury Fair 47

Shakespeare, William 18, 27, 45;
    Twelfth Night 37;
    King Lear 23;
    Hamlet 49;
    Much Ado about Nothing 32, 55;
    Measure for Measure 37
Shirley, James 32
Socrates 32
Spectator, The 45
Stanislavski 26
Steele, Richard 36;
    Commendatory verses 7, 59
Suckling, Sir John 34, 38–9, 40, 41

theatrical conventions 27, 58
theatrical modes, generic 7, 16, 27, 53, 55, 56–7
tragedy 13, 18, 52, 53
'types' 26, 47, 49, 50, 55

Voltaire 59, 61n.18

Waller, Edmund: *The Story of Phoebus and Daphne Applied* 41, 42
Wycherley, William 36;
    The Country Wife 9
wit 12, 13, 32, 33, 35, 37, 41, 42

Aliens for Breakfast

By Jonathan Etra
and Stephanie Spinner

Illustrated by Steve Björkman

A STEPPING STONE BOOK

Random House New York

Library of Congress Cataloging-in-Publication Data:
Etra, Jonathan. Aliens for breakfast / by Jonathan Etra and Stephanie Spinner. p. cm.—(A Stepping stone book) SUMMARY: Finding an intergalactic special agent in his cereal box, Richard joins in a fight to save Earth from the Dranes, one of whom is masquerading as a student in Richard's class. ISBN: 0-394-82093-2 (pbk.); 0-394-92093-7 (lib. bdg.) [1. Extraterrestrial beings—Fiction. 2. Science fiction.] I. Spinner, Stephanie. II. Title. PZ7.E854Al 1988 Fic—dc19 88-6653

30

To Mom—J. E.
To Calista—S. S.

1.

"Mom, I hate these sneakers." Richard Bickerstaff was getting dressed for school.

"You picked them out yourself last week, sweetie," his mother called from the kitchen.

"Last week they were okay. Today I hate them." Richard frowned at his feet. Why had he ever chosen these dumb black high-tops? He should have gotten red-leather running shoes like Dorf's. They were cool. But then, Dorf was cool. He had just moved here. He'd only been in Richard's class for two days, but already the other kids were imitating him.

They were copying his big smile, which showed off his perfect white teeth. And they were copying the way he dressed. On the first day he came to school, Dorf wore a red bowling shirt. It had his name, Dorf, spelled out on the pocket. The next day Richard's best friend, Henry, wore a bowling shirt. It had "Sylvia" stitched on the pocket. Everyone thought it was pretty great anyway.

Richard poked around in his closet, which was full of old Space Lords of Gygrax comics. He didn't have a bowling shirt and he knew it. But he looked anyway.

"Richard, finish dressing or you won't have time for breakfast," called his mother. "Hurry up. I have some new cereal for you to try."

Richard found a clean shirt and put it on. "I hate cereal," he said as he came into the kitchen. He scowled at his cereal bowl. It was full of strange little brightly colored shapes. "And this stuff is looking at me!" he added. All the strange little shapes had tiny silver eyes.

"It's called Alien Crisp," said his mother. She poured some milk into Richard's bowl. "I thought you'd like it, since you're such a sci-fi fan."

The little shapes seemed to grow as the milk touched them. Then everything in the bowl heaved and sighed.

Richard put down his spoon. "Mom, where did you find this stuff? It's alive!"

"Richard, your imagination is getting out of hand," said his mother. "It's a free sample. I found it in the mailbox."

"But it's moving!"

"The milk is making it move."

"The milk is standing still. The cereal is moving."

"Well, wait until it stops moving. Then eat it," said Mrs. Bickerstaff. "I have to get ready for work." Mrs. Bickerstaff was a lawyer. She almost never minded arguing. Except when she was in a hurry. Like now.

"I don't think it's cereal," muttered Richard as she hurried out of the kitchen. He picked up the cereal box. "Alien Crisp" it said on the front. "Crunchy, Munchy Aliens in a Box! Packed on the Planet Ganoob and Rushed Straight to You!"

Richard eyed his bowl. Everything in it had stopped moving. Then the milk gave a tiny splash. A round pink thing the color of chewed bubblegum started to climb up the side of the bowl. Amazed, Richard touched it with his spoon.

"Stop that!" The words came directly into Richard's head. He put his spoon down very quickly. Then he took off his glasses and wiped them on his shirt sleeve. But when he put them back on, the thing was still there.

"What do you think you're doing?" asked the voice.

"Uh, eating breakfast," answered Richard. Was a piece of cereal really talking to him?

It was. "I could use some breakfast myself," it said. It crawled out of the bowl and dropped onto the table. "The trip really took it out of me."

Richard finally found his voice. "Who are you?" he asked.

"Aric. Commander of the Interspace Brigade. Our goal: to wipe out cosmic troublemakers. Our record: ninety-eight percent success."

"You're an alien?" squeaked Richard. All those books he'd read about kids meeting aliens. And now it looked like it was happening to him. Him! Richard Bickerstaff!

"I am a Ganoobian," said Aric. *"You* are the alien."

I've got to be dreaming, thought Richard. He sometimes had very exciting dreams about space travel and large but friendly creatures from other planets who made him their leader.

"Well, come on! Do not just sit there!" said Aric. His voice was awfully loud for such a little thing. It boomed inside Richard's head. "Let us get going—I am busy. I have six other planets to save. Move it or lose it! Hup-hup-hup!"

"Wait a minute," said Richard. "Where are we going? Who are we fighting? What about school? I'm going to be late!"

"Hey—it is your planet," said Aric. "And you have been chosen to help me save it. But if you do not mind the Dranes taking over, hunky-dory." He started to climb back into Richard's cereal bowl.

"Who are the Dranes?" Richard wondered

if they were tiny and pink, like Aric.

"Space trash," said Aric. "Mean. Very mean. When the Dranes see a planet they like, they move in. Before the natives know it, their minds are mush. And the Dranes are in control. Forever!"

"And these, uh, Dranes. They're here?" asked Richard.

"Yes, they are here. Or to be precise, one is here. But one is more than enough. Dranes divide every four days. In a few weeks Earth will be knee-deep in them. Not a pretty sight."

"What does this Drane look like?" asked Richard.

"Well, Dranes can look like anything they want to. The one here has blond hair, blue eyes, and a smile no one can resist. He is in your class. He just showed up two days ago."

"Dorf? Dorf is an alien?" Richard was so excited he jumped out of his chair. He couldn't wait to tell Henry.

"My job is to get rid of the Drane before he divides," said Aric. Then, for a moment, he looked a little confused. "You have suitable weapons, of course."

"Weapons? All I've got is a water gun!" Somehow Richard knew that wouldn't be enough to stop a Drane.

Aric sat down on the table. "Maybe it is because I am not used to being soaked in milk," he said. "But I cannot remember—"

"You can't remember what?" asked Richard.

"The weapon to use against the Drane." Aric looked confused again.

"You mean you didn't bring weapons with you on your spaceship?"

"I have no ship," said the little alien.

"Then how did you get here?"

"I was freeze-dried and beamed from Ganoob in a cereal box. Fast and cheap," said Aric.

"Well, have them beam the right weapons down," said Richard.

"No, no—you do not understand," said Aric. "The weapon is here, on your planet. That is why I did not bring it. It is something found in many Earthling homes. Only, now—" He scratched his little pink head. "I cannot remember what it is!"

"Richard!" called Mrs. Bickerstaff. "School bus is here."

Richard scooped up his books and his lunchbox. "Look," he said. "I'm just a kid. And I have to go to school. You're the space warrior. You figure out what to do."

To Richard's surprise, Aric jumped onto his shoulder. "I am coming with you," he said. "Perhaps I will regain my memory when I see the Drane. Let us go forth!"

Richard plucked Aric off his shoulder. He tucked him gently into his shirt pocket. " 'Bye, Mom," he called. "I'm off to save the world."

"Have fun, sweetie," answered Mrs. Bickerstaff.

2.

Richard slid into his seat just as math was starting. He was under strict orders from Aric to act normal. "Do not let anyone know about me," he had told Richard on the way to school. "If the Drane finds out I am here, you can kiss this planet good-bye." So now Richard couldn't stare at Dorf, even though he wanted to. Instead he had to pretend that the only thing on his mind was the question Mrs. Marks was asking.

As usual, it was a hard one.

"Who knows how many ways we can make

change for a dollar?" she asked. She looked around the room slowly. Then she stared straight at Richard. His heart sank. "Richard?" she asked.

Richard knew you could get four quarters or ten dimes or a hundred pennies from a dollar. But that was too easy. This was a trick question with a trick answer. Only he didn't know the answer.

"Any ideas, Richard?" asked Mrs. Marks.

"Four?"

"Only four?"

"Five," he said quickly. He would have to bluff.

"Who thinks there are more?" asked Mrs. Marks.

"There must be at least ten," called Henry. He was good at trick questions. "What about a mixture of nickels, dimes, and pennies? Or nickels, quarters, and half-dollars?"

Half-dollars! thought Richard. I forgot those.

Then Dorf raised his hand. He had a big smile on his face. It showed off his perfect white teeth.

"Yes, Dorf?" said Mrs. Marks.

"There are two hundred ninety-two ways to change a dollar bill," said Dorf.

All the kids in the class stared at Dorf. How had he come up with that number?

"Good guess!" exclaimed Mrs. Marks.

"It's not a guess," said Dorf. "I figured it out last summer. On my computer."

"Well, you're very clever indeed," said Mrs. Marks. "Because that is the right answer. Can anyone explain why?" Her eyes moved up and down the rows. Richard tried to look invisible.

"You have pennies, nickels, dimes, quarters, and half-dollars," continued Dorf. "One hundred thirty-six coins in all. But you can mix them in all kinds of ways. Like five pennies, two dimes, five nickels, and a half-dollar. Or forty-five pennies, a nickel, and two quarters. There are hundreds of ways to do it. Two hundred ninety-two ways, to be exact," he finished smoothly.

Mrs. Marks didn't smile a lot. But she smiled now. And everyone in the class nodded, as if Dorf had just said something important and wonderful.

"He has begun to control their minds," said Aric. Richard jumped. For a moment he had forgotten about the alien in his pocket. Now he felt a thrill of alarm at Aric's words. What should he do?

"I told you before," said Aric's voice. "Just act normal. Do you understand?"

"Yes," said Richard silently, sensing that Aric could hear his thoughts. He felt hot and nervous. But at least math was over. He walked over to Henry's seat with his lunch box. They always traded sandwiches after math. Richard's mother made him tuna on whole wheat, which he hated. Henry's mother made him peanut butter and jelly, which *he* hated. So they traded. But when Richard got to Henry, Henry was already eating a sandwich. It looked like tuna fish. Dorf was sitting next to Henry. He was eating a sandwich, too. It looked like peanut butter and jelly.

"Hey!" said Richard. "Don't you want to trade?"

"Already have," said Henry, with his mouth full. "I traded with Dorf." His eyes, when he turned to Richard, looked funny. Almost as if they weren't focused right.

"But we always trade," said Richard.

"Here, Richard. Have half of mine," said Dorf. He offered his peanut butter and jelly with a smile.

"Do not look at his teeth." Aric's voice popped into Richard's mind. "They send out dangerous Drane rays that will bring you under his control. Look only into his eyes. They cannot harm you."

Richard took a deep breath and turned to Henry. "I hate tuna fish," he said. "And we always trade. How could you give my sandwich away?"

"It's not your sandwich. Anyway, Dorf got to me first," said Henry.

Richard sputtered with anger. "He's a—" Before he could say "Drane monster," Henry broke in.

"He's a great guy," said Henry. His mouth was still full of tuna fish. "He's got his own VCR and all the Mad Max tapes. And he's going to let me watch them on Saturday."

"Why don't you come too?" said Dorf. "A

whole bunch of kids from the class are coming. It'll be fun."

"I hate Mad Max!" said Richard, though this wasn't true. Then he saw that Henry was staring straight at Dorf. Right at Dorf's perfect smile. "And besides, I'm already busy," he finished weakly.

Then he sat down at his desk and looked blankly at his tuna sandwich. Earth is in BIG trouble, thought Richard Bickerstaff.

3.

All day Richard kept waiting for Aric to remember what the secret weapon was. But Aric didn't remember. Instead, he complained. He whined about having to stay in Richard's pocket. He made rude remarks about the classes he had to sit through. The only time he stopped complaining was during gym. Then he sat in the pocket of Richard's shorts and didn't make a sound. After gym he confessed that the smell of the basketball reminded him of Ingbar, his girlfriend on Ganoob.

But at last the school day was almost over.

Only art was left—Richard's favorite. He had been working for weeks on a drawing of the starship *Enterprise*. Now it was nearly finished. He settled down and got to work. Using a silver crayon, he drew in one last fin on the ship's side. "Isn't this great?" he asked Aric silently. Now that he knew he could send thoughts to the little alien, he was beginning to like it.

"Primitive," answered Aric. "Besides, interspace beaming is much cheaper."

"But what if you don't know exactly where you're going? Captain Kirk never has a destination. He spends his time on the *Enterprise* exploring space. Looking for strange new worlds."

"Get real. We have enough problems with the worlds we know already. Thanks to our friends the Dranes. In case you had forgotten."

Richard threw down his crayon. "How could I forget?" he said out loud. Too late, he remembered about sending the thought silently. What if someone in class heard him talking to himself? They would think he was crazy.

But no one even looked at him. His whole class was watching in silence as Dorf worked on his art project. Richard wondered why everyone was so impressed. After all, it was only a little white paper pyramid.

Mrs. Logan walked over to Dorf's desk. Dorf smiled one of his big smiles up at her. Her eyes got a little funny and glassy as she smiled back. "How beautiful!" she said to Dorf. "So three-dimensional!"

Henry was sitting next to Dorf. He stared at Dorf's pyramid for a long time. Then he stared at his own crayon drawing of two dinosaurs. Then he looked back at Dorf's pyramid again.

"Mrs. Logan, can I make something new?" he asked.

"What would you like to make, Henry?" asked Mrs. Logan.

"Uh, something three-dimensional. Like Dorf."

"What a nice idea!" said Mrs. Logan. "Of course! Go ahead."

Then Celia raised her hand. She was drawing a picture of dancing jellybeans. "Me, too," she said.

"Me, too," said Jennifer, Ruth, Philip, George, Leroy, Fawn, Dawn, Sean, and Tristram. Mrs. Logan looked pleased.

"If you'd all like to try something new, go right ahead," she said. The whole class got up. They walked to the supply table and took what was left of the white paper. Then they walked back to their seats and began making little white pyramids. They look like a bunch of robots, thought Richard.

Mrs. Logan came over to him. "Is something wrong?" she asked. "Don't you want to try something new too?"

"Not really," said Richard. "I haven't finished my starship yet."

Suddenly Mrs. Logan leaned closer. "What's that on your hand?" she asked. "Are you bleeding?"

Richard looked at his fingers. Yikes! The tips were bright red. Blood was oozing out from under his fingernails.

Richard grabbed his hand. "How did this happen? I didn't cut myself. I'm sure of it." Out of the corner of his eye he saw Dorf smile. Why?

"Do not look at his teeth," Aric told him. "Get out of class."

"You'd better go to the nurse," said Mrs. Logan. "She'll take care of you."

Richard stood, holding his hand up stiffly. Henry tore his eyes away from his pyramid. "Does it hurt?" he asked.

"Naw," said Richard, as if it were no big deal. The truth was, it didn't hurt. But it scared him. He knew he hadn't cut himself. Or had he?

"You did not," Aric told him on the way to the nurse's office. "I am sorry to have to break this to you. Dorf knows you are resisting him. So he is pulling a cheap Drane trick. He is rearranging your molecules. You are melting."

Richard stopped in his tracks. "Melting!"

"Well, dissolving is more like it," said Aric. "Your molecules are drifting apart. Slowly, of course."

They were outside the nurse's office. "This is terrible!" moaned Richard. How had he ever thought getting to know an alien would be fun? He felt like throwing up.

"It will not get much worse today or tomorrow," said Aric. "But I hope you do not have big plans for the weekend."

Richard whimpered.

"Once I remember the secret weapon, I can destroy Dorf. Then you will be fine," said Aric.

"But what if you *don't* remember?"

"If I do not remember," said Aric, "Earth will be so deep in Dranes that dissolving will be fun."

4.

Back in his own room after school, Richard looked at his bandaged fingers and tried to fight his panic. It wasn't easy. The fact that his fingertips had started to ache made it even harder. He thought of Dorf and shuddered.

"Listen, Aric," he said as calmly as he could. "Don't you think we should do some serious thinking about how to get Dorf? I mean, are you sure you don't have some superpowerful weapon stashed away? How about a sub-ion warp disrupter?" That was what the Space Lords of Gygrax used to blow away *their* enemies. It always worked. At least in the comics.

Aric jumped down off the stack of Yoda comics on Richard's shelf. He came to rest on the shoulders of a plastic King Kong. "Fancy weapons are too expensive for us,

Richard," he said. "The Interspace Brigade works on a very tight budget. We have 47 million planets to look after. Our yearly allowance is 249 billion daktils. That comes to about sixty-seven cents a planet."

"Sixty-seven cents to save Earth?" shouted Richard. "That's it?"

"That is plenty," said Aric. "We saved Zweeb for thirty-six cents two years ago. Dranes are a cheap menace. They can be fought with simple ingredients."

"Like WHAT??" yelled Richard.

"It will come to me," said Aric. "Just give me time."

"I can't believe it," said Richard. "My planet is being taken over by space hoodlums. I'm melting. And you, the *commander* of the Interspace Brigade, can't remember a simple ingredient!" His toes began to throb. Were they bleeding, like his fingers? He was too scared to take off his high-tops and look.

"I never said I was perfect!" snapped Aric. He slipped down off King Kong and started pacing. Then he stopped.

"Perhaps I could look around your house.

It might bring back my memory," he said.

"Sure. Where do you want to start? Garage? Kitchen? Bathroom?"

"I seem to remember that the substance can be eaten," said Aric. "Where do you store items of nourishment?"

"In the kitchen!" cried Richard. He grabbed Aric and headed down the hall.

Ten minutes later the Bickerstaff kitchen looked like a supermarket after an earthquake. The floor was covered with the contents of the refrigerator. Now Richard was emptying all the shelves. As he did, he showed each item to Aric. "This is peanut butter. This is hot chocolate. This is rice. These are graham crackers. These are pickles. These are soft drinks—Tab for Mom, Dr Pepper for me. Salt. Sugar. Tuna. See anything that will kill a Drane?"

"I do not think so," said Aric. He was sitting on a bunch of grapes. "And I really thought I would remember it right away."

"Dorf hasn't clouded your mind, has he?" asked Richard.

"This is an easy mission," said Aric. "I have

wiped out Dranes on lots of other planets. Though I have never been freeze-dried before. It must have shaken me up." He sighed. "We had better keep looking."

Richard got back to work. "How about these?" he asked. "Chocolate sprinkles for ice cream."

"Afraid not," said Aric. "Is this all?" The floor, the counters, the kitchen table and chairs were now covered with bottles, boxes, cans, and jars of food.

"Yes," said Richard.

"It is not here," said the alien. "Perhaps we

can search some other Earthling's home? One with a wider range of products?"

"We have the best kitchen on the planet," said Richard. "Mom buys everything. If it isn't here, I don't know where it could be." Then he had an idea. "Unless you want to go to the mall."

"Is there food at the mall?"

"Every fast food made in America."

"Then by all means let us go there," said Aric. "And quickly!"

5.

The mall was busy for a Thursday afternoon. Richard wondered why. Then he saw that one of the stores was having a promotion. It was for a new men's perfume called Sweat. A big fat man dressed like a wrestler was giving out free samples.

"Ugh! Why would anyone want to buy that stuff?" said Richard.

"To attract the female of the species, of course," said Aric.

"Girls? I can see spending money to keep them *away*," said Richard. "But I'd rather spend it on something cool. Like that." He pointed at a black satin baseball jacket in the window of a store. "I don't have enough money, though. Mom says maybe she'll get it for my next birthday. . . . Of course, I may never *have* another birthday." Richard's hands and feet were really hurting now.

"After we have destroyed the Drane, the Brigade may find some extra money to buy you a gift," said Aric. "You have earned something for all you have been through."

Aric sounded so sure of destroying Dorf that Richard felt a little better. "Gee, thanks—"

he started to say. But Aric interrupted him. "Great Ganoob!" cried the alien. "What is that?"

They were next to Mutant Splendor, a store that sold sci-fi games, books, toys, masks, and comics. It was just about Richard's favorite place in the whole world. Today the front of the store was taken up by a giant display of the Space Lords of Gygrax. The big plastic warriors had bright red wings, blue skin, and webbed feet. They were all snarling and holding laser swords, as if they were about to

attack. The display had sound effects, too—battle noises and strange space music.

Richard's mouth dropped open. For a second he forgot that his hands and feet hurt. This was awesome! Ten times better than the comic books!

But Aric didn't think so. "You call these Gygraxians?" he snapped. "They are a joke!"

"You mean there really is a planet Gygrax?" asked Richard.

"Of course," said Aric. "But Gygraxians do not have wings. They have fins. Not only that, their skin is orange, not blue. And they never fight. They are the biggest cowards in the galaxy. This is an outrage! I want to speak to the manager."

Aric started to hop out of Richard's pocket. Richard clamped a hand around him. "How can you get so upset about a bunch of stupid toys? Time is running out! You have to remember what the secret weapon is!" Was it Richard's imagination? Or was he beginning to feel wobbly? Maybe he was dissolving faster!

"Aric—" Richard went on. But then he froze.

Dorf and Henry were walking down the mall. They were dressed in the same red T-shirts and ripped jeans. Dorf was talking, and Henry was listening. He nodded his head at everything Dorf said. As Richard watched, they walked into Pizza World.

"Aric!" gasped Richard. "There they are! Dorf and Henry! Should we follow them, or what?"

"Follow," answered Aric.

"I've never trailed anybody before. What if they see us?"

"Do not worry," said Aric. "I will make us invisible."

"What! You can do that? How come you didn't do it before?"

"It is very expensive. Only for emergencies," said Aric. "And it only lasts ten minutes. Now let us go." He made a low humming sound that filled Richard's head for a moment. As he crossed over to Pizza World, Richard found himself humming too. He couldn't help himself.

When he reached for the door of the pizza parlor, Richard's hand disappeared. He looked down at his feet. They weren't there either. He was invisible!

6.

Being invisible was a little scary. Richard couldn't see or feel himself. So he couldn't tell where he began or ended. As he walked into Pizza World, he moved his arms and legs very slowly. He was hoping he wouldn't bump into anything. But even though he was really careful, he did. When he passed a table of four teenaged girls, he knocked over all their empty soda cups. Ice cubes and paper cups went flying. The girls screamed. Richard froze.

"Keep going!" Aric's voice boomed inside

Richard's head. "Have you never been invisible before?"

"Are you kidding?" answered Richard. "I'm human. We can't do that."

Aric gave a tiny snort. "Well, then," he said, "just sit down quietly. Try not to move around a lot. At least no one knows that we are here. The Drane is too busy with his food."

Dorf and Henry were sitting at a table covered with pizza pies and soft drinks. Richard held his breath. Then he sat down quietly beside Henry. It looked to Richard as if the pizzas were the house special—Death by Pizza. They had peas, carrots, onions, cheese, and wheat germ on them. Death by Pizzas were famous on the mall. No one had ever died from eating one. But people had come close.

"Just before Dranes divide they build up their power by eating a lot," said Aric. Richard's heart sank. There were seven pizzas on the table.

"Hey, these look really good!" Dorf licked his lips. "And isn't it great being here without that little nerd Richard?"

"Yeah. It's great, Dorf," said Henry in a spaced-out voice.

Richard felt like giving Dorf an invisible punch. "Maybe Dorf will die from the pizza," he said to Aric.

"No," said Aric. "The pizza will simply help him to divide faster."

Dorf picked up a glass shaker of red-hot pepper flakes and poured it all on one of the pizzas. He breathed in clouds of red dust. A big smile broke out over his face. Then he reached over to an empty table and grabbed another glass shaker. He poured pepper flakes over a second pizza.

Suddenly Dorf sprang up. He went from table to table, picking up all the pepper shakers. When his arms were full, he came back and sat down. He lined all the shakers up in front of him. Henry looked puzzled.

"What are you doing, Dorf?" he asked.

"Eating!" Dorf turned his widest smile on Henry. "I'm hungrier than I thought." One by one, he emptied all the shakers onto the pizzas. Henry gulped and turned green.

"What is in the bottles?" Aric asked Richard.

"Red-hot pepper flakes. The hottest stuff in the world. I can't believe he can eat all that and not explode."

"That is it!" shouted Aric. "Red pepper! I knew I would remember! That is the weapon!"

"Great!" Richard watched Dorf closely. He could hardly wait to see what the pepper flakes would do. But nothing happened. Dorf wasn't dying. He wasn't even looking sick. He was enjoying himself! He devoured slice after slice of the pizza, eating faster and faster.

Henry nibbled on the edge of a piece. Then he ran gasping for water. Dorf paid no attention. He ate and ate. His fair skin turned pink. His blue eyes flashed purple. A terrible greedy smile spread over his face, which was now covered with cheese and bits of carrot.

"How come it's not working, Aric?" asked Richard. "I mean, if it's the weapon, shouldn't he be getting weak or something?" Then Richard had an awful thought. What if Aric was wrong? What if the pepper flakes didn't work against Dorf?

"I am not wrong!" snapped Aric. Too late, Richard remembered that Aric could hear his thoughts. "It is all coming back to me now. The weapon is pepper flakes. Dranes cannot resist it. Once they start eating it they cannot stop. And then they explode."

"Then how come he's so happy?" asked Richard. If anything, Dorf looked stronger now than before.

"If he were eating just pepper flakes, he would indeed die soon," said Aric. "But he is eating pizza also. And that is giving him strength."

"What can we do?" asked Richard.

"We must feed him pepper flakes. And only pepper flakes," said Aric. "Enough to destroy him. And we must work quickly."

"Okay, I'll give it to him," said Richard. "Tomorrow. At school."

"Very good," said Aric.

By the time Henry came back, Dorf was on his last pizza. His face was bright red. Henry was staring into his empty cup. He looked sick.

"I don't feel so good," he said.

"Have another slice," said Dorf.

"Could we go home now? I think I'd better lie down."

"I'm almost finished. I feel really great. There's nothing like a pizza to get your blood flowing!" shouted Dorf. "How about running around the mall a few times?"

"Maybe later," mumbled Henry. Then he jumped up and ran off to the bathroom.

"We had better go," said Aric. "We are going to become visible again in about a minute."

Richard got up. Very carefully he made his way around the chairs and tables. He opened the front door and slid out of Pizza World. Then he headed back to Mutant Splendor. No one would notice if a kid and a tiny alien materialized there. They'd think it was some new game or promotion or something. And that was exactly what happened.

7.

The next morning Richard was up early. "Well, I guess today we save the universe," he said nervously. Aric was curled up in an orange Frisbee. He yawned and stretched.

"It is not the universe. Just your little home planet," he answered.

"I resent that," said Richard. He pulled his socks on over his bandaged feet. "If it's so small and unimportant, why are you here?" Richard's head was pounding. Was that part of melting too? In any case he was sick of Aric acting like such a know-it-all.

"All right. All right. Your planet *is* important. If the Dranes take over Earth, who knows what they will do next? But it is bad luck to brag, and worse manners. Your mother should have taught you that."

"She tried," said Richard. He went into his closet and pulled out a five-pound box of pepper flakes. He felt so weak that it was hard to lift the box. And he had spent $17.52 on it—his life savings.

"I sure hope this works," he said. "Do you think five pounds is enough?"

"It better be. Dorf will divide in exactly three hours and fourteen minutes. Then it is bye-bye, biosphere."

Richard shuddered. "I guess we'd better hurry," he said. "There's no place else to go if we mess up, is there?"

"Negatory, my friend," said Aric.

"Richard!" called Mrs. Bickerstaff. "Time to get up!"

Richard put Aric into his shirt pocket. He zipped the box of pepper flakes into his backpack. Then he walked into the kitchen. His mother, in her bathrobe, was opening and closing all the cabinets. "Where did the tea bags go?" she said. "I could swear they were in here yesterday."

"Gee, Mom, I sure don't know," said Richard. He and Aric had cleaned up the kitchen the afternoon before in a big hurry. They probably should have been more careful.

"You're up early this morning," said his mother. "How come? Something special going on at school?"

"No. Just felt like getting an early start," said Richard.

"Good for you! What would you like for breakfast? Some more of that nice new cereal?"

"No!" Richard croaked. He never wanted to see another box of Alien Crisp in his life.

Richard's mother peered at him. "Are you all right, honey?" she asked. "You look pale."

For a second Richard felt like a little kid again. He wished he could tell his mother everything. "I'm fine, Mom," he said. He sat down at the table. "Really."

"Well, at least have a good breakfast," said his mother. She smoothed back his hair. "How about an egg?"

"Sure," said Richard. To his mother's surprise he ate everything on his plate. Then he kissed her on the cheek and left to wait for the school bus right on time.

Richard was glad Henry wasn't on the bus. If he saw Henry, he wasn't sure he could keep quiet about Dorf. And he knew that saying anything would ruin Aric's mission. Then again, it was pretty clear that Henry was under Dorf's control. "He probably wouldn't believe me if I did tell him," thought Richard.

He walked into school and stood near the boys' bathroom. A second later Dorf and Henry came walking down the hall. They were both wearing red cowboy shirts and string ties. Dorf was talking, and Henry was nodding at everything he said. As usual.

"Remember. Do not look at Dorf's teeth when he smiles," said Aric. "And step back after you give him the flakes. Dranes can get violent before they explode."

Richard got hot. Then cold. Then slightly dizzy.

"Do not be afraid," said Aric.

"I'm not afraid. I'm terrified," said Richard. But even as he said it, he was stepping away from the wall. He stood in front of Dorf and Henry. "Hi, you guys," he said.

"Hi, Richard," said Dorf. "How are you doing? You don't look so good, buddy." Then he smiled one of his amazing smiles right at Richard. Just in time Richard remembered to look away. Then he said, "I was hoping I'd run into you before class, Dorf. I've got something I think you'll *really* like. Come on in here. I'll show it to you." He led them into the boys' bathroom, which was empty. Then he set his backpack down. It took all his strength to pull out the box of pepper flakes.

"Here. This is for you," Richard told Dorf. He opened the box. "Want some?"

Dorf looked at the pepper flakes. Suddenly his face was wet with sweat. He smiled a hungry smile. His breath came fast and hard, and his eyes gleamed. His face turned bright pink. He grabbed the box away from Richard. Then he poured a heap of pepper flakes into his hand. He stuffed it into his mouth as if he were eating popcorn. Only he didn't chew it. He simply swallowed it. Then he swallowed another handful. And another.

"Dorf! What are you doing?" cried Henry.

Dorf ignored him. His eyes turned bright purple. "More!" he gasped. He poured pepper flakes down his throat. "More!" The snaps on his cowboy shirt popped open. His chest was bright red. It started to steam. Henry jumped away. So did Richard. Now Dorf's eyes were bulging. He finished off the box and his skin went from red to purple. Then his hair started burning. It smelled horrible.

"Yikes!" said Richard. He grabbed Henry. They backed away toward the door.

Dorf began bubbling and popping. His clothes fell to the floor in a smoking heap. He stopped looking like a boy and started to look like a blob of live Silly Putty. Then he sprouted tentacles. There were dozens of them. They thrashed on the floor, making a loud hissing noise.

Richard felt something on his neck. He jumped. It was only Aric. He had climbed on Richard's shoulder to watch.

A horrible cry filled the bathroom. "You got me!" screamed Dorf. "Two more hours, and I would have started dividing. My clones would

have been all over your planet like ants on a candy bar! And then all you pathetic Earthlings would have been our slaves!" His tentacles flopped on the white floor.

"I hate to lose!" Dorf wailed at Richard. "I hope you flunk math and history. I hope you fail science and art and social studies and English and gym!"

Then he blew up.

8.

It had been a great day. Dorf was gone. Earth was saved. Richard had stopped melting. And he and Henry were friends again. In fact, now that Dorf was gone, everyone in Richard's class seemed a little friendlier. Richard didn't know why. It sure wasn't because anyone knew he'd saved the world.

The amazing thing was that no one even remembered Dorf anymore. Except for Henry. He was coming over later to spend the night. Richard planned to tell him all about the Dranes then.

The only bad thing about the day was that Aric was leaving.

"Can't you stick around for a while and hang out at the mall?" asked Richard. School was over, and he and Aric were back home. In a few minutes the Interspace Brigade was going to beam Aric back to Ganoob. He was leaving from the same place where he had landed—the Bickerstaff kitchen table.

"Sorry, the universe calls. Those Dranes never sleep," said Aric. "By the way, if you ever want to join the Brigade, just let me know."

"Would I get to fly around at light speed and blast monsters?" asked Richard. "Or wear a shiny red-and-blue uniform?"

"Mostly you have to travel fourth class in things like cereal boxes. And they make you wear baggy overalls, to blend in," sighed Aric.

"Oh," said Richard. That sounded almost as bad as school.

"The work is okay, though," added Aric. "Every now and then you run into a really brave freedom fighter. Someone who risks his life to save the world. That is truly satisfying."

It sounded like Aric was paying him a compliment. But Richard wasn't sure. "You mean me?" he asked.

"Absolutely."

"Wow. Thanks." He blushed. Then he asked, "Will I ever see you again?"

"Usually we do not go to a planet unless it is under attack," said Aric. "But sometimes we can work in a short stopover."

"That would be great! We could go to Mutant Splendor. And Pizza World. Just like old times."

"I would like that," said Aric. "And if you are ever near Ganoob, drop in. You would love Ingbar. Even if she is a girl Ganoobian."

Richard's heart sank. He knew he could never visit Ganoob. It was hard enough visiting his grandmother in California. But he managed to smile. "Sounds good. I'll try. Meanwhile, maybe you could send me a postcard sometime?"

"Maybe. Or maybe I will send you something else." By now Aric was standing on the salt shaker waiting for the Ganoobian transport beam. Suddenly he began to fade like a TV picture in a thunderstorm. "Goodbye,

Richard. Thank you." He waved.

" 'Bye, Aric. I'll miss you," said Richard. Then the alien was gone, and Richard started to cry.

The next morning Richard woke up suddenly. He sat up and rubbed his eyes. Henry opened his eyes at the same moment. He sat up too.

"Wow, Richard," he said. "I just had the most amazing dream. I don't know if it was all that stuff you told me about Aric, or what. But I dreamed I saw all these funny little pink creatures. They were bouncing up and down together in a big circle."

"Me too!" said Richard. "I had the same dream! Did you see two of them, sort of floating in the middle of the circle? Looking really, *really* happy?"

"Yeah. I wonder what was going on?" Henry yawned and got out of bed. He started to get dressed just as Mrs. Bickerstaff knocked on the door. "Rise and shine, boys!" she called. "Time to get up."

"I bet I know," said Richard. "I think it was

Aric's homecoming. And that was Ingbar with him in the circle." He smiled. "They sure looked like they were having a great time."

Richard opened his closet door. There on the floor was a brand-new black satin baseball jacket. On its back, in big gold letters, were the words "Interspace Brigade."

Richard picked it up and put it on. It was *really* cool. There was a note in one of the pockets.

"Thanks again," it said. "Wear this and have a pizza for me! See you, Aric."

About the Authors

JONATHAN ETRA was a humorist, playwright, and journalist, as well as a children's book author. He lived in New York City until his untimely death in 1991.

STEPHANIE SPINNER is a children's book editor and writer. She lives in New York City and has always wanted to go to Ganoob.

About the Illustrator

STEVE BJÖRKMAN is an illustrator whose work often appears in magazines. He notes, "I have been drawing ever since I was a kid. I was often reprimanded for doodling in class and now find it a great relief to do a drawing without having to hide it from the teacher." Steve Björkman lives in Irvine, California.